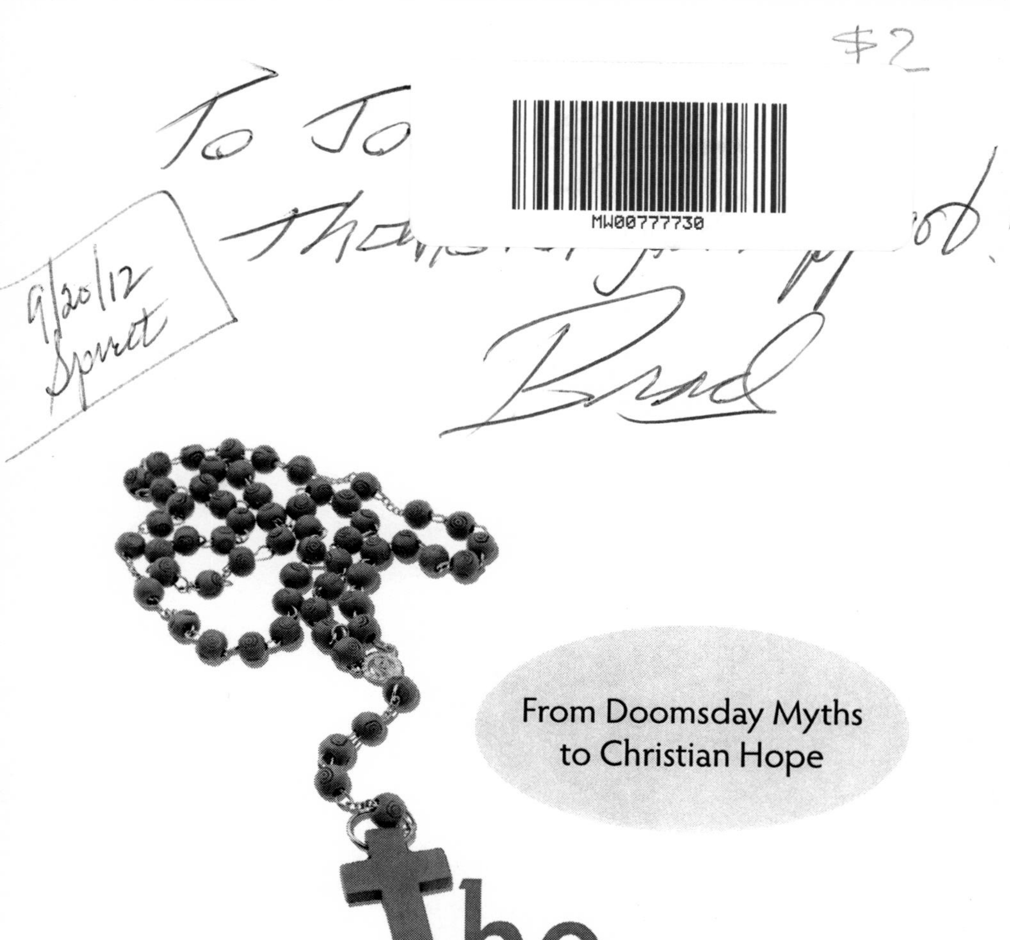

From Doomsday Myths to Christian Hope

The Future?

Brad McIntyre

The Future? From Doomsday Myths to Christian Hope

Published by Wheatmark®
1760 East River Road, Suite 145
Tucson, Arizona 85718 U.S.A.
www.wheatmark.com

ISBN: 978-1-60494-750-2
LCCN: 2012932668

To my mother, Gloria,
who nurtured biblical hope,
who completed the race and now rests in peace.

The message of Christianity is not Christianity,
but the New Reality.
--Paul Tillich

Contents

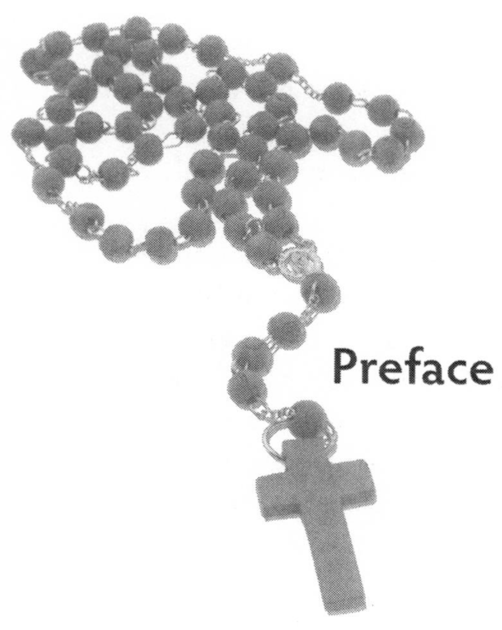

Preface

The world was supposed to end in 2011—twice.

Harold Camping, a 90-year-old California radio evangelist and Bible prophecy specialist, believed the Rapture would occur on May 21, 2011. Then he changed the date to October 21, 2011. Wrong again. After the second failure of his prediction, Camping issued a vague apology to his followers and summarized the debacle by saying, "We are simply learning" (Waits 2011).

There is a slow learning curve for doomsday prophets. Some never seem to learn, and many people are deceived and become disillusioned. Our age is supposedly enlightened and rational, yet millions of Christians believe the most bizarre things about the end of the world. I have personal experience with this.

I was raised in a church founded on paper-thin prognostications about the end of the world. I attended "prophecy seminars" where traveling evangelists, dressed in dark blue suits, preached on Daniel and Revelation. They strung Bible verses into long necklaces of nebulous theories about Armageddon, Antichrist, and the Millennium. These preachers paid little attention to the historical context of a passage of scripture or to what it might have meant to the original author. It was obvious to them that the Book of Revelation was written just for us and we were the only ones who understood it.

I viewed charts with pictures of beasts and dragons and timelines. The Pope was Antichrist, and we were taught to be suspicious of Catholics. Signs and wonders allegedly exploded all around us. Every day the time clock ticked. We lived in the shadow of the Second Coming. I was told by one church member to not even think about going to college because the world would end before I graduated. Soon there would be a movement to create a one-world government, then Armageddon, and then Christ would return just in the nick of time.

We flew on the wings of apocalyptic fantasies and sang happy hymns played on a Hammond organ. Our little band of hopefuls represented American middle class decency merged with prophetic glitz. Best of all, we had the future figured out and no one else did.

I look back on that experience, over forty years ago, and can identify at least three features: *supernaturalism*, *apocalypticism*, and *sectarian certitude*. We were an apocalyptic sect. The apocalyptic worldview is entirely supernaturalistic and otherworldly. If taken literally, apocalyptic prophecies can become absurd. People begin to think they have decoded the details about the future. They engage in biblical arithmetic about coming events. The stage is set for wild predictions, doomsday theology, and all sorts of eschatological mischief.

Eventually I left that church, but I never rejected Christian hope in God's coming future. I realized that the Bible describes "the end" in symbols and myths. The New Testament is full of mythological symbols about the end of the world. I was able to affirm Christian eschatology and Christian hope by reinterpreting the Bible's eschatological symbols and myths.

This book is a series of biblical essays focused on eschatology and Christian hope. It is a book of interpretations. I am offering what I hope is a positive alternative to doomsday theology and apocalyptic literalism. The symbols of Christian hope must be interpreted and translated into a modern idiom. The message about God's coming future must be shared, but it must also be translated or it remains foreign. Every translation is an interpretation. With this in mind, I invite the reader to join me in a process of interpreting Christian hope for today based on the eschatological message of the Bible.

My deepest conviction is that God remains "the Alpha and the Omega, the first and the last, the beginning and the end" (Rev 22:13).

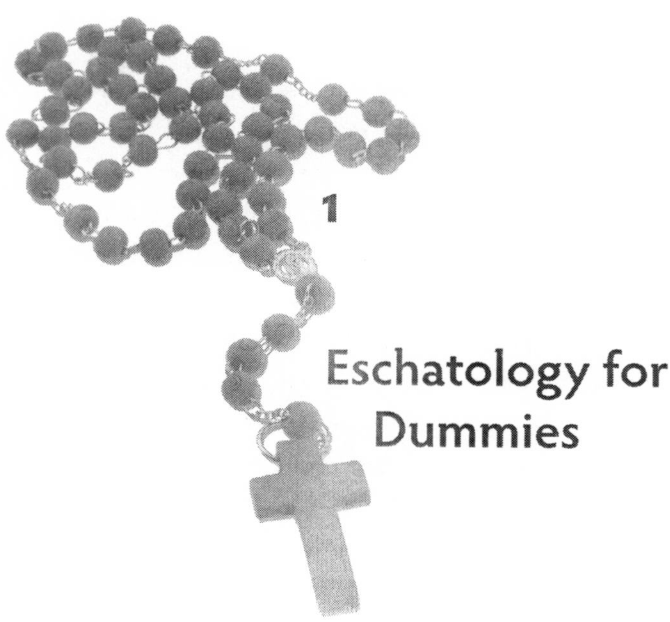

1 Eschatology for Dummies

Reflection on God's coming future is called "eschatology" or "the last things." Eschatology is about the hope of salvation at the end of time.

The Greek word *eschaton* refers to "the end" or "the final thing." The goal of eschatology is the kingdom of God, which means the end of history as we know it. At the center of this hope is Jesus Christ crucified, resurrected, and coming again in power and glory. Christ will bring in the new age of God's kingdom. Then he will deliver the kingdom over to God the Father, and God will be all in all. No more evil, sin, suffering, pain, injustice, persecution, or death. Rather, there will be peace, love, and righteousness, Eden restored, the New Creation, and eternal life.

Sounds pretty good. But how do we talk about this hope? What images and symbols do we use? How does the Bible express this hope and are we obligated to accept biblical cosmology?

Christianity began as an apocalyptic movement within Judaism. The New Testament is not a humanistic document; it does not teach that the kingdom of God comes by natural means or gradual development within history. As important as social ethics are, the human project to create Utopia on earth is not the biblical idea of the kingdom of God. Moreover, we are confronted with *the apocalyptic aroma of the New Testament.* Apocalyptic is a way of talking about the end times, the conclusion of temporal history. The dominant form of New Testament eschatology is apocalyptic. Both Jesus and Paul embraced apocalyptic eschatology to a great degree. I will describe the characteristics of the apocalyptic eschatology in detail in the next chapter. For now, let me describe a main feature of apocalyptic, namely, the cataclysmic end of the world.

Apocalyptic envisions an abrupt end to life as we know it. This cataclysmic ending will be preceded by dark days of evil, suffering, war, violence, immorality, and anarchy. But a miraculous divine intervention will bring an end to this present evil age and inaugurate the Age to Come. This transition will come suddenly and unexpectedly when Christ returns in power and glory. There is no hope for the world apart from God's supernatural salvation. Christians are to stay occupied while they wait by doing good deeds, but there should be no false hopes that human initiatives can save the world. The future kingdom of God will be brought about by God alone, supernaturally. Earthly kingdoms and nations and political systems will be annihilated. Everything will come to a fiery end by means of a cosmic firestorm. Those who are not on God's side will suffer eternal damnation. This is the apocalyptic worldview. This eschatological hope is the framework for the New Testament.

There are many warnings in the New Testament against date-setting. No one knows the hour! The message is, "Keep awake! Be ready! Watch!" The present is a time of *decision.* There is no time to fritter away one's life on lesser things. Jesus is coming soon! Get ready!

The above apocalyptic scenario is entirely *mythological.* It is grounded in a mythological worldview derived from Jewish apocalyptic. We are left with the task of interpreting myth and finding the abiding spiritual truth embedded in the mythological symbolism.

This interpretive process is called "demythologizing," and it is essential for translating Christian hope for modern people. We need not repudiate mythological symbolism, but we must interpret it.

What does myth mean?

Myth is not a derogatory term. It does not mean falsehood. Religious myth is a way of talking about the invisible world and spiritual realities. How do we explain the existence of evil? We tell a story. How do we talk about the end of the world? We tell a story. Myth is storytelling. Yet the stories express deep truths about human existence and the meaning of life. For example, the story of Adam and Eve is a mythological depiction of "the Fall." It points to the fact that we are not what we were created to be, we have fallen away from our essential nature and need redemption. Our existence in time does not reflect what we essentially are. The theological word for this is *sin*, and the solution is salvation. Adam and Eve were not real people living at a particular time and in a particular place. But the myth of the Fall is central to our understanding of ourselves and God's redeeming love.

Christian eschatology expresses spiritual truths in mythological language. We can talk about the end of the world only in pictures, symbols, and stories. Religious myth objectifies what is essentially invisible and spiritual.

We must distinguish between two words: *eschata* and *eschaton*. The first word, *eschata*, refers to all the details associated with the end—the objectifications of spiritual realities. Unfortunately, these details get more air time than the main event itself, the *eschaton*. For example, many Christians get lost in the details of Armageddon and Antichrist and the seven last plagues. They get caught up in a play-by-play drama of last day events and yet miss the big picture. There is no consensus about details and I doubt there ever will be. Does there need to be? No. Speculation about last day events is a futile endeavor that often leads to nonsense.

On the other hand, we can count on the *eschaton*: The End. This is the New Age, the final state of things. The *eschaton* is beyond human experience. We can describe it only in metaphors, symbols, and images. We can talk about the end of the world only symbolically. This requires careful interpretation or hermeneutics. The *eschaton* is the final goal of history and the aim of human destiny. What God has started, God will finish. This is the abiding message of Christian eschatology and the source of Christian hope.

Forms of Eschatology

There are three forms of eschatology:

- Individual eschatology (Eternal Life)
- Communal eschatology (Kingdom of God)
- Cosmic eschatology (New Creation)

These are the three great symbols of Christian eschatology: *Eternal Life, Kingdom of God, and New Creation.* Each refers to a specific way of expressing hope in God's coming future. Each is pointing to the same reality but saying it in a different way or with a different emphasis.

Individual eschatology. This is the personalistic form of eschatological hope usually expressed as "eternal life." It is about responding to the grace of God in Jesus Christ and knowing you are at peace with the Lord and that your eternal destiny is secure. Individual eschatology is about the salvation of souls. People must *choose.* They must repent and be converted and live a transformed life. Such a person can die in hope of the resurrection at "the last day." This is the evangelical side of Christian faith. God is in the business of saving souls one at a time. The gospel must be preached throughout the world in order to save souls. This belief can bring the assurance at the time of death that one is going to "be with the Lord." This is the idea behind individual eschatology.

Yet the Bible emphasizes the salvation of the individual only in relation to a saved community of faith, namely, the elect people of God. This brings us to communal eschatology.

Communal eschatology. God chooses a community of salvation to bear witness to his salvation. Individuals are important, of course, but God works primarily through his "elect." In this theology, God works by means of a covenant, first with Israel and then with the church. Israel was called by God to be "a light to the nations." The Christian church was "elected" to bear witness to the Messiah, Jesus Christ. The Old Testament prophets spoke to Israel as a nation, as God's people. In the New Testament the church supplants Israel as the new people of God, although debate still continues as to the destiny of literal Israel. The main thrust of communal eschatology is that a person is saved by becoming a member of the people of God. God remains faithful to his covenant despite the unfaithfulness of his people. This social aspect of salvation is expressed in the symbol "the kingdom of God." God's kingdom is what the world will look like when God's people are at last victorious and God rules over all.

Cosmic eschatology. New Creation is the most universal symbol of all. Here is the big picture of the end. Beyond saving souls and a community of believers, God wants to remake the whole creation from top to bottom. Jesus becomes the Cosmic Christ, far above all principalities and powers. This Cosmic Christ exerts his cosmic authority to vanquish all lesser powers and to renew all things. The end is a lot like the beginning. Eschatology and creation are intimately related. We look for "a new heavens and a new earth." This is the New Creation.

It boils down to hope—hope for individuals who are committed to the kingdom of God and the universal renewal of all things. This is the ultimate vision of Christian eschatology. But it cannot be hope in this or that scheme of last day events or hope that certain Bible prophecies will be literally fulfilled. It is not hope in doctrines about the end of the world but hope in God alone and in God's coming future. It is as the Apostle Paul said in First Corinthians:

> For our knowledge is partial, and our prophecy is partial,

> but when the complete comes, the partial will come to an end . . . For now we see in a mirror, dimly, but then we will see face to face. Now I know only in part; then I will know fully, even as I have been fully known. (1 Cor 13:9, 12)

In another passage, Paul describes the inner groaning of all creation for the final fulfillment of God's dream for this world. We ourselves groan inwardly, but all creation groans, too, and longs to be delivered from its "bondage to decay" and to experience ultimate freedom. "For in hope we were saved. Now hope that is seen is not hope. For who hopes for what is seen? But if we hope for what we do not see, we wait for it with patience" (Rom 8:24-25).

It is important to take apocalyptic seriously but not literally. It is even more important to maintain eschatological hope. This hope can be summarized this way: *God will finish what God has begun.* How, I don't know. When, I don't know. But how and when are not as important as what and whom. The earth as we know it cannot last forever. What then? The message of Christian eschatology is that in the end there is not nothing, there is God. God is the end-point of existence. God's mysterious future draws us forward even now as we plod along from year to year. God's mysterious future is coming at us. As Paul Tillich wrote, "The divine aim will finally come to prevail" (Tillich 1967:334).

Apocalyptic visionaries offered a time-bound picture of the end. Our modern age, I believe, has rendered apocalyptic mythology obsolete. Yet there is no reason to abandon Christian hope and the urgency to live for God and God's coming kingdom. We can still maintain a responsible and realistic hope in eternal life, the kingdom of God, and the New Creation. This is the essence of Christian eschatology and theme of this book.

2

God in History?

I maintain that *Christian hope is hope in the coming God, but this God is already present in history now.* I will begin by discussing the concept of biblical time. Then we will look at apocalyptic eschatology, prophetic eschatology, and the nature of Christian hope.

Making Sense of Time

You know what time it is, how it is now the moment for you to wake from sleep.

--Romans 13:11

Biblical time is linear. In linear time, history is a succession of unrepeatable moments and unrepeatable lives. We live one personal life and only one. This life is the only time we have to work out our destiny. There is no coming back at a later time to "get it right." This gives the Bible a sense of urgency and seriousness. People must *decide* for or against God and God's kingdom. Both

Judaism and Islam share this view of time, since these religions also share a common heritage with the Bible. Judaism, Christianity, and Islam are the great religions of linear time. All three religions believe that history is moving forward toward a goal: *the final rule of God over all.*

The biblical timeline moves from history before history (creation stories) to salvation history. The Bible is holy history, not secular history. It is history with an agenda. The agenda of biblical history is God's plan for history. History in the Bible is shaped by faith: Israel's faith (Old Testament) and Christian faith (New Testament). It is assumed that history has a *telos* or aim. History is telescopic; it envisions an end-point to all things. God is carrying out a plan for history. God is fulfilling his purposes in history. God is in charge of history.

The main theme of the Bible is *promise and fulfillment.* Biblical history is the story of the faithful God who makes good on his promises. Everything is headed to an ultimate goal when God at last brings everything in creation to fulfillment. Various symbols describe this goal: eternal life, the kingdom of God, the New Creation. As we have seen in the previous chapter, eternal life is the symbol for individual salvation, the kingdom of God symbolizes the historical/political expression of salvation, and New Creation expresses the cosmic dimension of salvation. These symbols point to the final goal of history: the establishment of God's rule over all creation.

To envision time as a linear process directed by God to a purposeful end is called "eschatology." Jesus was an eschatological prophet announcing the arrival of the kingdom of God (see Chapter 6). Jesus believed the end was near. The first Christians believed the end would occur in their lifetime. Early Christian faith was eschatological faith in the coming God, who will fulfill his promises. Eschatology is not an appendix to Christian theology but is its heartbeat. Wolfhart Pannenberg writes,

> Because God and his lordship form the central content of eschatological salvation, eschatology is not just the subject of a single chapter in Christian theology; it determines the perspective of Christian doctrine as a whole. (Pannenberg 1998, 3:531)

God's future shapes the Christian understanding of the present and of time itself. The coming kingdom of God is the framework of the Christian worldview. God's future is the final horizon of the meaning of our existence. This future has been expressed in many ways. It is ineffable. It is not accessible to normal human experience. This is why God's future can be described only through metaphors, pictures, and myths. This leads us to a type of literature and worldview called "apocalyptic eschatology."

Apocalyptic Eschatology

> *And I saw a beast rising out of the sea, having ten horns and seven heads; and on its horns were ten crowns, and on its heads were blasphemous names.*
>
> *--Revelation 13:1*

Apocalyptic comes from the Greek word *apocalypsis*, meaning "to reveal or disclose." Apocalyptic visionaries and writers believe they have received special revelations from God about the future. Apocalyptic is a mythology and an ideology about the end-times. More precisely, it is ideology in the form of mythology—images, pictures, and calculations about the end of the world. Apocalyptic literature is intended to bring hope to God's persecuted people who are alienated from the dominant society. It is written to bring hope to the oppressed and downtrodden people of God, the saints.

Christian apocalyptic is derived from Jewish apocalyptic, which inherited it from Persian sources. The mythological figure of Satan, for example, did not originate in Israel but in Mesopotamia.

There is no evidence that the Israelites believed in the existence of a supernatural being named Satan until after the Babylonian exile (6th cent. B.C.). Jewish faith is not apocalyptic by nature. Jewish apocalyptic was imported from a foreign source. Christianity borrowed apocalyptic imagery from Judaism to express Christian hope in the coming of Christ. To a certain extent, Jesus himself shared an apocalyptic worldview and was influenced by apocalyptic thinking.

When life is bleak and God's people are being crushed, apocalyptic literature offers a view of history. It pulls back the veil and reveals that God is the ruler of history and will bring everything to a conclusion. Goodness and righteousness will ultimately triumph over evil, and God's "remnant people" will be saved. Apocalyptic is an interpretation of history from the perspective of the underdog. The focus of apocalyptic is the future. The present age is devoid of God and under the control of Satan. This brings us to three main features of an apocalyptic worldview: *cosmic dualism*, *pessimism*, and *the two ages* (Rist 1962).

(1) *Cosmic Dualism*. The entire cosmos (heaven and earth) is caught up in a cosmic controversy between God and Satan. History is a battle between the forces of Good and Evil. There is no middle ground. God's angels are counterbalanced by Satan's angels; the true Christ is opposed by the Antichrist (an incarnation of Satan). History is the stage for this warfare and every individual is caught up in it. Evil powers are everywhere, but good powers will win out in the end.

(2) *Pessimism*. Apocalyptic writers see no hope for history as we know it. No efforts to make the world a better place will succeed. Their vision is entirely pessimistic. The world in its present form is lost. Time is expiring and things are so corrupt that only God can save the situation. One must

place all hope in God's coming kingdom. It is no surprise that a persecuted and alienated religious group would view the world in this manner. Such groups have no access to the power structures of society. They are outsiders. To the persecuted and oppressed, the world is not a friendly place, and reforming the world is not an option. "Rescue from on high" is the only option.

(3) *The Two Ages*. Cosmic dualism and pessimism lead inevitably to belief in the two ages: the present evil age and the age to come. The present age is passing away. God's new age—the Messianic Age—is coming soon. World history is divided in two. Apocalyptic writers emphasize the age to come when God will destroy Satan and evil and set up his reign. Then God's people will be saved and enjoy all the blessings of paradise.

There are secondary features of apocalyptic, such as, visions and dreams, symbolic animals and numbers, angels and demons, and lists of woes. Apocalyptic literature appeals to the oppressed and reveals a God who in the end will bring history to a glorious conclusion, a new heaven and a new earth (Rev 21:1). "And God will wipe away every tear from their eyes" (Rev 7:17).

Violent eruption and cosmic cataclysm are features of how the end will come about, according to the apocalyptic writers and preachers. There will be a violent break with the past. Time will end with a bang! God will appear with vengeance to slay the unjust, and with compassion to save the saints. But all of this will come from outside of history. Whether we call it "the day of the Lord" or "the coming of the Son of Man" or "the end of the world," salvation will come from outside of history and bring an end to history as a temporal process.

It is only natural to ask when all of these things will take place. Thus, apocalyptic enters into predictions and calculations about the end times. Apocalyptic preachers talk about signs of the end. Current events are viewed through the lens of Bible prophecies. It is believed by many that prophecies are being fulfilled every day. The end of the world is just around the corner.

But is it?

Isn't the apocalyptic worldview a time-conditioned worldview? Can it be artificially reawakened in our times? Are we required to do the number crunching of apocalyptic math? The apocalyptic imagination is provocative, but is it not also pedantic and grindingly monotonous? C. H. Dodd observes that apocalyptic is derivative by nature. Apocalyptic writers borrow heavily from each other and keep recycling certain features that are the common property of the genre. Certain plots recur again and again, "rather like the stock plots of an Elizabethan theatrical company" (Dodd 1960:180). One gets the impression that apocalyptic writers are not as original as they would have us believe. This applies to the author of the Book of Revelation. John the Revelator was familiar with Jewish apocalyptic literature, as well as the Old Testament. Revelation is deeply Jewish with a Christian twist: Jesus Christ has been inserted into a Jewish apocalyptic format. Revelation is "Christianized" Jewish apocalyptic, largely derivative.

Is apocalyptic eschatology necessary? Is it possible to embrace a fervent hope in the coming God without the apocalyptic worldview? It might be necessary to do this in light of apocalyptic extremists and doomsday theology. We are in need of "the responsible use of apocalyptic," since apocalyptic fanaticism has often resulted in millennial zealotry and violence (Jewitt & Lawrence 2003:147-48).

It is important to note that eschatology is not necessarily apocalyptic. Apocalyptic is a type of eschatology. It is one way (and one way only) of interpreting God in history. Most of the Bible is not apocalyptic, but it is eschatological. Apocalyptic is a type of literature embedded in the Bible. This brings us to "prophetic eschatology."

Prophetic Eschatology

He has helped his servant Israel, in remembrance of his mercy, according to the promise he made to our ancestors, to Abraham and his descendants forever.

--Luke 1:54-55

The Christian gospel is aimed at bringing the nations to "the obedience of faith" (Rom 1:6). What kind of faith is this?

First, it is a faith for all nations, for "Jews, Greeks, and barbarians." This is a universal gospel that embraces all humanity, not just one little apocalyptic sect within humanity. Nor is it a gospel for a select group of initiates schooled in "secret knowledge" like the Gnostics. There is nothing esoteric about the Christian message. Nor is it a mystical message for those who are able to detach from the world and work themselves up the ladder toward full "enlightenment" through rigorous meditation practices. Rather, the gospel is a message for all people of all times. It is out there for all to *hear.*

Second, Christian faith is a "theology of the Word." The gospel is a straightforward proclamation of salvation. The message is proclaimed; people hear it and respond. "Faith comes through what is heard, and what is heard comes through the message about Christ" (Rom 10:17). "We declare to you what was from the beginning, what we have heard, what we have seen with our eyes, what we have looked at and touched with our hands, concerning the word of life" (1 Jn 1:1). Spirit-inspired proclamation results in Spirit-filled faith. The human heart and mind, moved by the Spirit of God, take hold of the message of salvation—the message about Jesus Christ.

Third, Christian faith is faith in the God of history. This is not the God of deism who is remote and distant, watching passively from on high. This is the God who gets his hands dirty in the stuff of history. Christian faith is fundamental trust that God has done something, is doing something now, and will do something in the future. Past, present, and future all belong to God. This God is moving history along to an appointed end: *fulfillment.* This is the God of Israel and of Jesus Christ. This is the God who speaks through the prophets. "Concerning this salvation, the prophets who prophesied of the grace that was to be yours made careful search and inquiry" (1 Pt 1:10).

The prophetic Word is about God's righteousness. "The righteousness of God" is God's deliverance, the time when God acts to vindicate his people and bring salvation to the nations. God acts to fulfill the promises he has made to Israel and to the human race. Christian faith views the cross and resurrection of Jesus Christ as "the turning point of the ages." These two events are inseparable. They are the ultimate events of God's righteousness. For it is through the death and resurrection of God's Messiah that the "new age" at last breaks through in power. We have all been living in "the last days" since the resurrection. We are living in the messianic age. The powers of the coming age are here now and will be fulfilled in the future. That future, God's future, is already on the way. Because of this, Christian faith is always *advent faith.*

This is prophetic eschatology.

Jesus arrived on the scene announcing the advent of the kingdom, "The time is fulfilled, and the kingdom of God has come near! Repent and believe the good news!" (Mk 1:15). Here is a positive, hopeful message that calls for a response. But there is also an implied warning, "If you don't repent, there is no hope for you!" This is the two-edged sword the prophet wields. The arrival of the kingdom of God is good news for the poor, the sick, the friendless, the oppressed, the needy, and all who repent. It is bad news for the hard-hearted.

The voice of the prophet is not always an apocalyptic voice. The prophet is called by God to speak the message of God to the people of God and to the nations. The message calls for repentance. Whereas apocalyptic focuses on the futility of history, the prophet focuses on the transfiguration of history through the Spirit and the

Word. The apocalyptic writers call for people to separate themselves from this evil age, but the prophet calls for conversion. He or she plunges into the midst of history and announces the advent of God's kingdom. There might even be hope that if people respond to God's call, God himself will relent. God pleads with humanity through the prophet, and the prophet confronts humanity with God's coming future.

Prophetic eschatology is grounded in history and envisions the transfiguration of history. Its model is not annihilation but conversion. But be warned! Those who will not receive the message will be excluded from God's future (Final Judgment). The prophets speak the Word of God in real history, in concrete situations, to real people. I believe Jesus was this type of prophet, despite apocalyptic elements in his message (many of which were added later). Jesus was not a prognosticator. He spent no time calculating the end. Rather, he was announcing the good news that the kingdom was drawing near. God's approaching future meant that the present was transformed. Because God is on the way, the present has taken on fresh significance.

Prophetic eschatology is faith in the God who makes good on his promises. Promise and fulfillment is the theme. Moreover, God's salvation is not limited to the distant future following Armageddon. God is in history now, working out his purposes now. This is why Jesus prayed, "Your kingdom come, your will be done on earth, as it is in heaven." He meant now, not a million years from now.

No Utopias, but No Despair

In gathering the weeds you would uproot the wheat with them. Let both of them grow until the harvest.

--Matthew 13:29-30

According to Jesus, the wheat and the weeds must grow together in the same field "until the harvest" (Mt 13:30). It would be wonderful if the field was pure and filled only with wheat. But the field is an ambiguous mixture of wheat and weeds, and so is history.

This should caution us against all utopias and millenarian movements, whether religious or secular. Watch out for any movement that tries to establish God's kingdom on earth. No ideal society is free of ambiguity. Utopia literally means "no place." There will never come a time when the field will be wheat only. There will never come a time when human beings create the millennial kingdom on earth. There is nothing wrong with trying to make the world a better place. Christians are called to follow Jesus and his example. This includes taking a stand for social justice. It means resisting oppression, poverty, discrimination, and violence. To follow Jesus is to resist all systems of domination that dehumanize people or promote themselves as world redeemers. No utopias! The wheat and weeds exist together until the final harvest.

In the end, God alone brings the kingdom and the New Creation: "See, I am making all things new!" (Rev 21:5). The new does not arise from the old. The new is really new in the sense of surprise and exceeding our expectations. The eschatological promise is not fulfilled by evolutionary forces or historical developments. God's promise always "overspills" history. History cannot contain it. God never exhausts himself in one particular historical reality (Moltmann 1991:103). Even the proclamation of Jesus pointed to greater fulfillment in the future. There is more to come. God will accomplish "abundantly far more than all we can ask or imagine" (Eph 3:20). The promise of God continues to expand with every fragmented fulfillment in history until the end.

Summing up, to envision time as a linear process directed by God to a purposeful end is called *eschatology*. The heart of Christian faith is eschatology, faith in the God who was and is and is to come: "Holy, holy, holy, the Lord God the Almighty, who was and is and is to come!" (Rev 4:8). Christian faith is trust in the God who makes promises and keeps them. Christian hope is hope in the God who is present now and who is on the way.

No utopias, but no despair either. God can be trusted to finish what he has started.

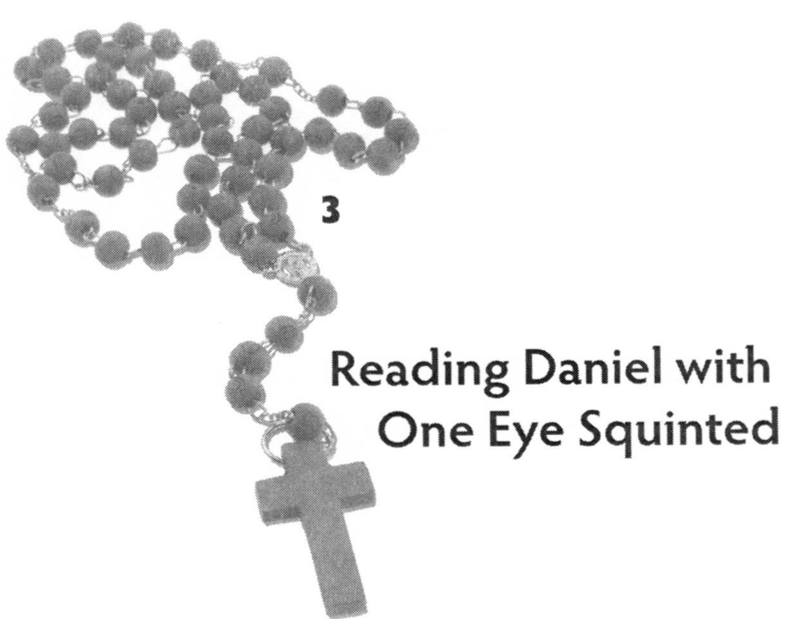

3

Reading Daniel with One Eye Squinted

In the 19th century, William Miller (1782-1849), a farmer in upstate New York, calculated the year Christ would return using biblical arithmetic based on the Book of Daniel. Miller was a student of Bible prophecy. He believed Christ would return in 1843. When that didn't happen, he went back to Daniel, tweaked this and that, and changed the date to 1844. Wrong again. Miller retired from the prediction business soon after this, in humiliation. Miller's followers (Millerites) eventually became the Seventh-day Adventist Church. Adventists still base their identity to a large degree on Daniel. Apocalyptic prophecies and biblical arithmetic are central to Adventism.

Daniel has always been important to apocalyptic prognosticators. Along with Revelation, Daniel has been used to spin fantastic scenarios of last day events. But should such apocalyptic speculation be central to Christianity? Can Daniel be rescued from abuse by those who use it to make predictions about coming events? Is Daniel, in fact, a play-by-play forecast of future events?

Is Daniel about *us* and *our times*? No . . . and yes, but only to a certain extent, and only if we read Daniel with historical realism and a certain amount of healthy skepticism. Judaism as a whole is less interested in the Book of Daniel than are Christians, as pointed out by Stanley B. Frost,

> Orthodox Judaism has evinced only a moderate enthusiasm for the book, partly because of its attempt to calculate the time of the end, and partly because of the general Jewish reaction against apocalyptic; but the Christian church has never been in any doubt as to its prophetic character and value. (Frost 1962, 1:762)

One might wish that Christians would have more doubts about Daniel than they do, or at least doubts about Daniel's interpreters. We need to read Daniel respectfully, but with one eye squinted.

Locating the Book Historically

The book of Daniel did not fall out of the sky; it is not from beyond time. Daniel arose within history in order to address a concrete historical situation. What was that situation? Here is where historical realism comes in.

Daniel is pacifist resistance literature written for Jews in response to a national crisis of faith in the 2nd century B.C. (around 165 B.C.). I am referring to the Seleucid Empire after Alexander the Great and under the rule of Antiochus IV Epiphanes (r. 175-164 B.C.). He was also called "Antiochus the Madman." The Seleucids controlled Judea at this time, and Antiochus attempted to destroy the Jewish religion. He pursued a relentless program of Hellenization, banned Sabbath-keeping and circumcision, outlawed the Torah, and in December 167 B.C., set up a statue of Zeus in the Jerusalem temple. This is "the abomination of desolation" referred to by Daniel (8:13; 9:27; 11:31; 12:11). Daniel was written during this time of trouble to bring consolation and courage to beleaguered

Jews who were standing firm for their faith and, in some cases, being martyred.

Probably the best sources for this period of Jewish history are I-II Maccabees, found in the Apocrypha. The despotic rule of Antiochus IV is described in detail in I Maccabees 1:10-34. But Antiochus is also described in the cryptic apocalyptic language of Daniel,

> He shall speak words against the Most High, shall wear out the holy ones of the Most High, and shall attempt to change the sacred seasons and the law; and they shall be given into his power for a time, two times, and half a time. (Dan 7:25)
>
> A King of bold countenance shall arise, skilled in intrigue. He shall grow strong in power, shall cause fearful destruction, and shall succeed in what he does. He shall destroy the powerful and the people of the holy ones . . . But he shall be broken, and not by human hands. (Dan 8:23-25)

"Not by human hands" implies a pacifist stance. According to Daniel, Antiochus IV would not be overthrown by violent insurrection but by divine intervention from on high. For a limited time—three and a half years—the Jews would suffer and some of them would be martyred. But soon God would act to deliver them!

The dating of Daniel during the reign of Antiochus is not a new idea. As John J. Collins points out,

> Already in antiquity, critics inferred that the Book of Daniel was not written in the Babylonian period, but in the time of persecution, before the actual death of Antiochus Epiphanes became known in Jerusalem. The lengthy predictions are *ex eventu*, or prophecy after the fact. The accuracy of these predictions helps reassure the reader that the part still unfulfilled (the end of the persecution and the resurrection) is also reliable. The purpose of the revelations is to

assure the persecuted Jews that their deliverance is at hand. (Collins 2005, 1:415)

We begin, then, by placing the book of Daniel in a period of persecution. The visions and dreams are intended to bring hope that God will soon act to deliver his people. The author of Daniel did not see history continuing on indefinitely.

A Philosophy of History

Daniel 1-6 includes six edifying legends about Daniel and his friends. These stories take place in Babylon in the 6th century B.C. The Jews are in exile. They must find a way to live in a pagan culture and yet stay true to their Jewish faith. Daniel is a young Jewish hero who demonstrates courage and fidelity to God, even to the Jewish food laws (Dan 1). Five of the stories revolve around Daniel, and one story relates to his brave friends, Shadrach, Meshach, and Abednego, who are thrown into a fiery furnace but are miraculously rescued (Dan 3). Daniel is also thrown into the lion's den; he, too, is miraculously rescued (Dan 6). We also read the story of Belshazzar's feast and "the handwriting on the wall," one of my favorite stories in the Bible (Dan 5).

Young Daniel is wise and is gifted with the Spirit of God. He is clairvoyant and can interpret dreams. Daniel makes a name for himself by interpreting the dream of King Nebuchadnezzar (Daniel 2). The emphasis is on Daniel as a revealer of mysteries (Dan 2:28, 30, 47). Subsequently, he and his friends are elevated to important positions in the state—observant Jews who succeed in a pagan society. These stories are inspirational and function as *hagiography*, not reliable history. Nevertheless, the same theme runs through them all: Nonviolent resistance and God's sovereign control over history.

The main challenge in Daniel is found in chapters 7-12. There is a distinct break as the book shifts from hagiography to apocalyptic visions. Beginning with Daniel 7, we find the man Daniel receiving four visions. The visions include beasts, cryptic numbers, obscure predictions, mysteries, and secrets about the future. Furthermore, the figure of "the Son of Man," so often referred to in the Gospels, is taken from Daniel, as is the phrase "the abomination of desolation"—another apocalyptic term that has generated much debate.

Daniel contains an important philosophy of history. The main theme of Daniel is *God's sovereign control over history.* This theme runs throughout the book, both the legends and the apocalyptic sections. Yet Daniel's view of history is different than the view of the traditional prophets of Israel. The book's apocalyptic approach to history must be distinguished from the prophetic approach.

Gerhard von Rad classifies apocalyptic literature as part of Israel's wisdom tradition, not its prophetic tradition (see Chapter Two). The Old Testament prophets were not a group of esoteric seers revealing secret knowledge about the future. They were not primarily a literary group. As von Rad comments, "The prophetic message, which was proclaimed absolutely openly, has nothing to do with esoteric knowledge" (Von Rad 1962, 2:308).

For apocalyptic writers, however, the future can be known only by the initiated, by those who can decode the "mysteries." Daniel fits into this category. Daniel is not classical prophecy; it is apocalypticism, written for the chosen few who can penetrate God's secrets about the future. In apocalyptic literature there is always a secret revealed, usually from an angel to a seer. In Daniel, there are visitations from angels. There are dreams and visions. These are literary devices heightening drama and emphasizing that the knowledge shared is divine knowledge, not mere human knowledge.

One wonders how many Jews living in Judea in the 2nd century B.C. embraced the apocalyptic worldview. To what extent did these esoteric writings influence the average Jew on the street? Norman K. Gottwald suggests that there were likely various apocalyptic communities in Palestine at that time, diverse in class and status. Because of persecution, hardship, and deprivation, any Jew might be swayed to become an apocalyptist. We might even imagine an apocalyptic movement made up of alienated prophets, disillusioned wise men, and some disaffected priests (Gottwald 1985:590). It is also likely that Daniel (especially Dan 7-12) was composed by a number of authors belonging to the Jewish Hasidim, "the pious ones" (Hartman & Di Lella 1978:43-5). This was a pacifist group committed to strict observance of the Torah.

What is the secret knowledge Daniel is sharing? It is a particular view of history. The prophets expected God to act within history, but for Daniel God acts from *outside of history.* God controls history and determines all outcomes, yet in the end, the kingdom of God is a supernatural, transcendent event that comes from above. Whereas the prophets called for social justice and social reforms in obedience to God, Daniel refers to neither. Daniel never calls for social righteousness or for revolt. God's persecuted people are not called to take up arms, and neither are they spurred on to change society. There is no hope for history or for society whatsoever. What is needed is a supernatural intervention from outside of history. The only thing people can do is to wait for the clock to strike and for the hour to come when God's eternal decree pronounces judgment and "the holy ones" gain possession of the kingdom (Dan 7:22).

In Daniel, divine transcendence eclipses divine immanence. The pendulum swings all the way over to the otherworldly realm. Kingdoms come and kingdoms go, history is bankrupt, but God's kingdom will soon arrive from beyond history and will last forever. This theme is expressed by King Nebuchadnezzar when he finally sees the light:

> I blessed the Most High and praised and honored the one who lives forever. For his sovereignty is an everlasting sovereignty, and his kingdom endures from generation to generation. All the inhabitants of the earth are accounted as nothing, and he does what he wills with the host of heaven

> and the inhabitants of the earth. There is no one who can stay his hand or say to him, "What are you doing?" (Dan 4:34-35)

To summarize, Daniel is concerned about political empires; more specifically, about the *duration* of empires and how long empires last before God topples them. This is why Daniel is concerned about numbers and calculating the time of the end. How much longer until God delivers his people from godless empires and arrogant rulers?

In Daniel's view, all earthly kingdoms are straw dogs destined to rise and fall. God establishes kingdoms and judges, punishes, and replaces kingdoms. The handwriting is on the wall: "Mene, Mene, Tekel, and Parsin." Or, "God has numbered the days of your kingdom and brought it to an end . . . you have been weighed on the scales and found wanting" (Dan 5:24-28). Thus, the book of Daniel is pacifist political theology. It is a statement against all human kingdoms, empires, and nations. The only legitimate kingdom is God's kingdom.

Let's Do the Numbers

Reading Daniel with one eye squinted means taking seriously its historical context and not turning Daniel into biblical arithmetic. In Daniel, Jewish history becomes cosmic history, and secular history becomes eschatology. A local political crisis is magnified into cosmic warfare. That is how apocalyptic works.

We have identified the crisis as the desolation of the Jerusalem temple by Antiochus IV Epiphanes. This becomes evident in Daniel 7-12. These apocalyptic chapters are later additions to the earlier folktales about Daniel and his friends. Various authors contributed, but each of them was focused on the desolation of the temple. Consider the following verses,

> For how long is this vision considering the regular burnt offering, the transgression that makes desolate, and the giving over of the sanctuary to be trampled? (Dan 8:13)
>
> Lord, let your face shine upon your desolated sanctuary. (Dan 9:17)
>
> And the troops of the prince who is to come shall destroy the city and the sanctuary. Its end shall come with a flood, and to the end there shall be war. Desolations are decreed. He shall make a strong covenant with many for one week, and for half of the week he shall make sacrifice and offering cease; and in their place shall be an abomination that desolates. (Dan 9:26-27)
>
> Forces sent by him shall occupy and profane the temple and fortress. They shall abolish the regular burnt offering and set up the abomination that makes desolate. (Dan 11:31)

Again, these verses are written by apocalyptists during the reign of Antiochus. The driving question behind their concern is, *How long?* How much longer is God going to let this sacrilege continue? How long until God acts to destroy this anti-God power and re-establish the temple sacrifices and Israel? The authors don't offer an exact date. Let's look at the numbers.

Daniel 7-12 is obsessed with calculating the duration of the persecution under Antiochus IV—"the appalling abomination." We find three and half years (7:25; 9:27; 12:7), 1,150 days or 2,300 evenings and mornings (8:14), 1,290 days (12:11), and 1,335 days (12:12). Though the numbers don't tally exactly, the duration of time is a little more than three years. Daniel "predicts" that the end will come in about three years. The end would mean the establishment of the kingdom of God, the salvation of Israel, and the restoration of the temple sacrifices.

This, I believe, is the central meaning of the complicated vision of "the seventy weeks" found in Daniel 9:24-27,

> Seventy weeks are decreed for your people and your holy city: to finish the transgression, to put an end to sin, and to atone for iniquity, to bring in everlasting righteousness, to seal both vision and prophet, and to anoint a most holy place. Know therefore and understand: from the time that the word went out to restore and rebuild Jerusalem until the time of an anointed prince, there shall be seven weeks; and for sixty-two weeks it shall be built again with streets and moat, but in a troubled time. After the sixty-two weeks, an anointed one shall be cut off and shall have nothing, and the troops of the prince who is to come shall destroy the city and the sanctuary. Its end shall come with a flood, and to the end there shall be war. Desolations are decreed. He shall make a strong covenant with many for one week, and for half of the week he shall make sacrifice and offering cease; and in their place shall be an abomination that desolates, until the decreed end is poured out upon the desolator.

This passage is notoriously difficult to interpret and there is no consensus on its meaning. Many Christian commentators see the seventy weeks (490 years) as a reference to Christ, the "anointed one" who was "cut off" (crucified). Calculations move from the decree to rebuild the temple (the dates for this decree are disputed) to the coming of Jesus. But is this the case? Are the seventy weeks of Daniel 9 a prediction of the ministry and crucifixion of Christ? Might this be reading too much into the text?

From a historical perspective, the seventy weeks are a general reference to Israel's history from Persian times up to Antiochus IV. The reference to the sacrifice and offering being abolished refers to Antiochus desecrating the temple. The vision is meant to bring hope to Jews living during 167-164 B.C. The message is, "Hang on! In a short time the reign of terror will be over!" And it was. The temple was rededicated by Judas Maccabeus in December 164 B.C.; Antiochus died in Persia on a military campaign that year.

Nevertheless, the numbers in any scenario of Daniel 9:24-27 do not add up exactly. The seventy weeks remain a bear trap for exegetes. How can such a cryptic passage function as a reliable basis of Christian belief? It can't.

At any rate, Daniel 7-12 is an apocalyptic description of "the abomination of desolation" or "the appalling sacrilege that leaves the temple desolate of God's presence." These chapters attempt to offer hope that the persecution will soon be over and God's people—the Jews—will be delivered from their distress. Daniel is about the salvation of the Jews. It is Jewish triumphalism in the same way that the Book of Revelation is Christian triumphalism. In Daniel, the coming kingdom of God is equated with deliverance for the Jews and the reestablishment of Israel.

Later interpreters, however, applied Daniel's visions to their own times. The symbolism and themes of Daniel recapitulated. Three eschatological symbols are,

- The Son of Man
- The abomination of desolation
- The resurrection of the dead at the end of the age

These three symbols were appropriated by early Christian interpreters and "Christianized." I will offer a brief analysis of these symbols in the next and final section of this essay.

Christianizing Daniel

There is nothing explicitly Christian about the book of Daniel. It is a Jewish book. As Christians, we are left with a hermeneutical challenge, namely, what is theologically relevant in Daniel for us?

I have already pointed out that Daniel is not predictive prophecy but prophecy after the event. Yet Daniel is eschatology, and eschatology is about the coming kingdom of God at the end of time. On this point, Daniel remains relevant for Christians, since this is the theme of New Testament theology. Early Christianity was an apocalyptic movement within Judaism. Jesus shared an apocalyptic worldview and believed in the eschatological drama at the end of the age, including the coming of the Son of Man, the resurrection, the final judgment.

Regarding the symbol of "the Son of Man," Daniel does not predict the coming of the Messiah. The key passage is Daniel 7:13-14,

> As I watched in the night visions, I saw one like a human being coming with the clouds of heaven. And he came to the Ancient One and was presented before him. To him was given dominion and glory and kingship, that all peoples, nations, and languages should serve him. His dominion is an everlasting dominion that shall not pass away, and his kingship is one that shall never be destroyed.

These verses are not describing the Second Coming of Christ. Rather, they portray *Israel* as the one who comes in human form into the presence of God to receive the kingdom. The "son of man" in Daniel 7 is a personalized image of corporate Israel. I concur with the observation, "In Daniel 7 the symbolic manlike figure has no messianic meaning, except perhaps as connected with messianism in the broad sense, i.e., with God's plan of salvation for his Chosen People" (Hartman & Di Lella 1978:219).

But Daniel 7 has a messianic flair. The passage points to a future time when the kingdom will be given over to God's people, the Jews. This hope became a messianic hope within Judaism, especially in Jewish apocalyptic literature. By the time of Jesus, many Jews looked for a transcendent Son of Man or a heavenly Messiah who would descend from heaven and deliver God's people from Roman rule. Jewish hope for a political King David was transformed into a spiritual hope for a heavenly Messiah. We can place Jesus and the early Christians in this group of apocalyptic hopefuls. The Gospels refer to Jesus as the Son of Man. Jesus described in colorful detail the coming of the Son of Man (cf. Matt 24:30-31; Mk 13:26-27). Eventually in Christian circles, the coming of the Son of Man became the Second Coming of Christ.

Once again, "the abomination of desolation" in Daniel refers to Antiochus IV setting up an altar to the Greek god Zeus in the Jerusalem temple in 167 B.C. Christian interpreters used this phrase to refer to the destruction of the temple in 70 A.D. by the Roman general Titus. In Matthew we read, "So when you see the desolating sacrilege standing in the holy place, as was spoken of by the prophet Daniel, (let the reader understand), then those in Judea must flee to the mountains" (Matt 24:15-16). This apocalyptic portion of Matthew is discussing the destruction of Jerusalem and the end of the age. Here we see how Christian apocalyptic gathered themes from Jewish apocalyptic and reapplied them in light of the coming of Christ. Today the concept of "the desolating sacrilege" has lost its symbolic power and is nonexistent in Christian circles, except in Christian apocalyptic movements such as premillennial dispensationalism.

The most powerful eschatological idea inherited from Daniel is the resurrection of the dead at the end of the age. In Daniel 12:2-3 we read,

> Many of those who sleep in the dust of the earth shall awake, some to everlasting life, and some to shame and everlasting contempt. Those who are wise shall shine like the brightness of the sky, and those who lead many to righteousness, like the stars forever and ever.

Here is the clearest statement of the resurrection found in the Old Testament. It includes the resurrection of the righteous and the unrighteous, based on the idea of eternal rewards. It is intended to bring hope to the Jewish martyrs and dread to those Jews who compromised their faith through accommodation to Hellenism or who caved in under persecution.

The resurrection is also a statement about *theodicy,* that is, God's justice. There is a reward for those who stand firm for God and who give their lives in the cause of God. God will make sure they are rewarded with eternal life. This issue, obviously, concerned Jews in Daniel's time, Jews who had been massacred by Antiochus. A just God will make sure that the righteous are rewarded and the perpetrators of violence and bloodshed will be punished. This is the main thrust of the idea of the resurrection of the dead in apocalyptic literature.

By the time of Jesus, many Jews believed in the resurrection of the dead at the end of the age, including the Pharisees. They looked forward to a future time when God would raise the dead and judge the world in righteousness. This is an apocalyptic idea. Christian belief in the resurrection of the dead can be traced back to Jesus himself and to even more ancient sources, such as the apocalyptic visions of Daniel.

The resurrection continues to be central to Christian faith and theology. It is certainly more central to Christian identity than the Son of Man image and the abomination of desolation. We rarely hear about Jesus as the Son of Man. That title was far too Jewish and became untranslatable into Greek culture. The "desolating sacrilege" is also a Jewish idea related exclusively to the temple. We cannot artificially reawaken these apocalyptic symbols by merely resolving to do so. Nor should we resurrect the mythology of Daniel by turning Daniel into a description of future events that will soon take place. Daniel is prophecy *after the fact.*

The theological relevance of Daniel for Christians is not its apocalyptic images and calculations but its eschatology. In Daniel, Christians can find an emphasis on God's plan for the world and the aim of history, as well as the promise of resurrection at the end of time. From Daniel, Christians learn that the arrogant kingdoms of the world will be crushed "not by human hands" but by the power of God alone.

Finally, reading Daniel with one eye squinted and from the

perspective of Christian faith, points us in the direction of God's ultimate and decisive revelation, Jesus Christ himself. This revelation was preceded by a period of preparation during which Judaism developed the idea of a coming messiah. This is the topic of the next chapter.

4

Messianic Hope in Judaism

The idea of the Messiah drives the hope of Judaism to a certain extent and Christianity to a large extent. Not all Jews believe in the Messiah or are "messianic." On the other hand, being a Christian means being messianic and embracing an unambiguous messianic hope. For Christians, Jesus is the Messiah, God's anointed one, the Christ. This is the normative center of Christian faith.

Judaism is not a messianic religion; faith in the coming of the Messiah forms only one strand of Jewish faith. Judaism has never proclaimed an official theology of the Messiah. There is no infallible Jewish dogma about the messianic age. The Messiah has meant different things to different Jews, depending on what rabbi one follows or what Jewish denomination one belongs to. Belief in the Messiah runs deep in some Jewish circles, but there is wide diversity within Judaism regarding the Messiah and the messianic age.

Messiah means hope, and hope leans into fulfillment, and fulfillment presupposes eschatology: *a new future quite different than the present state of things.* Eschatology means God's future, God's kingdom, the final aim of history. All these images cluster around the idea of the Messiah. Messianic hope is advent hope. It is hope in the Messiah who is on his way and who inaugurates "the ideal time."

How did the idea of the Messiah evolve in Judaism?

One could say that the idea of the Messiah is the most important contribution of Judaism to the world religions. Yet Israel was not always messianic. We do not find the idea of the Messiah in the stories about Abraham, Isaac, Jacob, Joseph, or Moses. There was no messianic hope during the early tribal confederacy of Joshua and the judges. When Samuel was called to his prophetic role, messianism did not exist in Israel. We must look to *David* and the establishment of the monarchy to find the roots of the Messiah. Messianism developed out of monarchy, and the Messiah was originally a political idea:

- Messiah as the ideal king of the end-times, anointed by God and called to restore the Davidic kingdom to greatness.

But there is another view of the Messiah: the eschatological Messiah. This position developed later in Judaism and was popular in the first century A.D. when Jesus lived. Thus, we see two pictures of the Messiah: *political and eschatological.* One is nationalistic and earthly; the other is universal and otherworldly. This counterbalance has played itself out in Jewish and Christian history.

Messianism has produced utopian dreams, revolutionary political movements, terrorist attacks, false messiahs, painful disappointments, and it fuels the current conflict in the Middle East. Messianism is an idea that can be perverted and used as a lethal weapon. Jewish theologian, David Ariel, comments, "Historically, we have had disastrous experiences with messianic activism" (Ariel 1995:246). Handle with care! This seems to be the warning regarding faith in the Messiah. Where did this faith begin? It began a long time ago with King David.

From Tribal Confederacy to Monarchy

I will tell of the decree of the Lord: He said to me, "You are my son; today I have begotten you."

--Psalm 2:7

The beginning of the monarchy in Israel was not ideal. The history of the kings of Israel is ambivalent at best and disastrous at worst. Was monarchy good for Israel? Wasn't the monarchy (after David) one failure after another? Didn't the monarchy lead eventually to the total destruction of Israel as a nation? Are not most of the prophets in the Old Testament anti-monarchical?

Israel's demand for a king led to monarchy in the late 11th century B.C. This was a major paradigm shift from a tribal confederacy under the direct rule of Yahweh to a centralized state apparatus under the kingship of David. The only way the Davidic monarchy could continue to legitimate its authority was to say that God was behind it. King and priests combined to solidify the Davidic dynasty. Royal ideology co-opted God into its program. Later, the traditions about David were shaped by editors to portray David as the greatest ruler who ever lived and whose dynasty would last forever. But we must read between the lines to find the truth.

The people forced the issue of kingship upon Samuel (1 Sam 8). Samuel did not want a king, and he said Yahweh didn't want a king either. But Samuel was old. He gave in to the people's request against his will. Kingship began with conflict and an opposition party. Not everyone sang praises to the king. Not everyone wanted to give a tenth of their crops to a king. Not everyone wanted centralized authority or a standing army or Jerusalem as the national capital. Monarchy can be expensive and oppressive. Wasn't Yahweh king of Israel? Don't royal dynasties tend to safeguard their own power base?

At any rate, Israel became a monarchy under David, who ruled from 1004 to 965 B.C. The first king, Saul, was inept and lasted only eight years. David ruled forty years, and he remains the ideal king for Jews to this day. Jewish nationalistic hopes are predicated upon the ideal kingdom and another ideal king like David. This hope became messianic: hope in a future Messiah anointed to liberate Israel from its enemies, just like David.

Political realities led to monarchy. A centralized power base and a strong military leader were necessary if Israel was to survive and not be annihilated by the Philistines (Kung 1992:67). The external threats were too great. Temporary charismatic leaders and an ad hoc militia could not defend Israel any longer. Kingship was a purely political decision. David began as defender of Israel and became a conquering warrior. Israel became expansionist and entered its glory years, but the glory years did not last for long.

We see in the Old Testament an intentional emphasis on the king as God's "anointed" (*mashiach*) endowed with the spirit of the Lord. The lineage of David is everlasting. The king is "God's son" (Ps 2:7). This does not imply essential divinity but election and intimacy with God. As "the son of God," the king functions as God's chosen representative filled with God's spirit. The "royal psalms" elevate David and his descendents to supreme status (see Psalms 2, 18, 20, 21, 45, 72, 89, 101, 110, and 132). The oracle of Nathan the prophet to David is central to royal ideology:

> I will appoint a place for my people Israel and will plant them, so that they may live in their own place, and be disturbed no more . . . Moreover the Lord declares to you that the Lord will make you a dynasty. When your days are fulfilled and you lie down with your ancestors, I will raise up your offspring after you, who shall come forth from your body, and I will establish his kingdom . . . Your dynasty and your kingdom shall be made sure forever before me; your throne shall be established forever. (2 Samuel 7:10-17)

These verses provide the paradigm for Jewish political messianism: the hope for an ideal Davidic king and nationalistic dreams. Embedded in this prophecy is an eschatological vision. The coming offspring of David was transformed into the coming Messiah of the end-times. This person is not an apocalyptic savior, nor a preexistent divine being. The Messiah to come is a descendent of David and is a human being—not superman, but almost.

The basic role of the Messiah is:

- To bring an end to suffering, humiliation, and foreign domination
- To gather the exiles back to Jerusalem
- To restore the nation Israel, a literal kingdom with land

Messianic hope in Judaism was intensified by various national disasters over the centuries. Perhaps the greatest disaster was the destruction of the Second Temple in 70 A.D. by the Romans. This, along with the rise of Christianity, led Jewish rabbis to focus more on the Messiah. The temple was gone, the priesthood was gone, and the nation was gone. The need for deliverance was acute. These rabbis systematized the various theories of the Messiah and codified them in the Mishnah (200 A.D.). The Christian claim that Jesus was the Messiah forced the messianic question onto Judaism as never before. These two forces—the destruction of the Second Temple and the rise of Christianity—led the rabbis to formulate a more intentional messianic theology (Werblowsky 1987).

Years later, in 1172 A.D., the Jewish philosopher and commentator Maimonides (1135-1204), wrote a famous letter to the Jews in Yemen who were being persecuted by a fanatical Muslim ruler and led astray by another man claiming to be the Messiah. He said,

> You write about a certain man who makes the rounds of the cities of Yemen, claiming to be Mashiach [Messiah]. Let me assure you that I am not surprised at him. Without a doubt, the man is insane. . . . Don't you know that a person

> who falsely pretends to be a prophet must be put to death for having assumed this great title, just as a person who prophesied in the name of idols must be executed? (Finkel 1994:39)

Maimonides proceeded to list examples of many other false messiahs from former times. He warned the Jewish community in Yemen that just prior to the messianic age many false messiahs will arise. They are to remember that when he appears, the Messiah will be "superior to any human being," as it says in Isaiah 9:6 and 11:2-3. These passages describe the Messiah as "Wonderful Counselor, Mighty God, Everlasting Father, Prince of Peace," as one who is full of wisdom, understanding, knowledge, and the fear of the Lord. To Maimonides, the Messiah is a human being of the lineage of David who is God's anointed king of Israel, yet he is superior to all other human beings.

Maimonedes wrote, "The most distinctive feature of the Messianic Age will be our freedom from foreign domination, which prevents us from fulfilling all the commandments." Other tasks include rebuilding the temple in Jerusalem, reestablishing the Torah as the normative rule for Jewish life, establishing justice and righteousness, rooting out idolatry and false worship, and bringing about peace (*shalom*). This, in the view of many Jews, is the messianic age. It will occur on earth and last for a distinct period of time within history. How long will it last? Again, there is more diversity than dogma on this point. The key teaching, however, is that the messianic age is a transitional period leading to "the age to come." It will last anywhere from 40 to 2000 years (Ariel 1995:229). Maimonides taught that the Messiah would die a natural death, as all human beings do, and be succeeded by a number of sons (Finkel 1994).

Messianic hope in a future Davidic king is summarized in creedal form by Maimonedes and is called the *Ani Maamin* prayer: "I believe with complete faith in the coming of the Messiah and, even if he should tarry, yet I will wait for him." Jews being led to the Nazi gas chambers sang this prayer as an expression of their deepest hope.

The Eschatological Messiah

> *And in the days of those kings the God of heaven will set up a kingdom that shall never be destroyed, nor shall this kingdom be left to another people.*
>
> --*Daniel 2:44*

We now move into a more complicated development in Israelite faith: *the eschatological Messiah.* Hope in a political Messiah is the oldest messianic hope in Judaism and the easiest to grasp. But the idea of an eschatological Messiah of the end-times is more obscure and controversial. This hope arose after the fall of the monarchy. Certain Jews gave up waiting for a new David, gave up hoping for a political Messiah, and put their trust in salvation from on high. The salvation of history would come from beyond history. Political hope became transcendent hope.

Messianic hope is a subordinate theme in Israelite faith. The Messiah is not the central idea of the Old Testament. The heart of Israel's identity is the creed, *"Yahweh is God, and Israel is his people."* Election and covenant form the basis of Judaism, not messianic dreams. Jewish expectation is based on God's covenant faithfulness. God is the one who redeems Israel: "You are my people" (Isa 51:16).

Furthermore, during and after the Babylonian captivity, the salvation of the Lord was described as a "new creation." Consider the following verses from Isaiah,

> Do not remember the former things, or consider the things of old. I am about to do a new thing; now it springs forth, do you not perceive it? I will make a way in the wilderness and rivers in the desert. (Isa 43:18-19)

> For I am about to create new heavens and a new earth; the former things shall not be remembered or come to mind. But be glad and rejoice forever in what I am creating; for I am about to create Jerusalem as a joy, and its people as a delight. (Isa 65:17-18; see also Isa 45:7-8, 12, 18; 48:12-13; 51:3)

Here Israel's salvation is nothing less than cosmic: the entire world and all nature are saved by Yahweh. Cosmic suffering requires a cosmic solution. Human effort alone is not enough. It is a universal vision of the end-times that takes us far beyond the temporal vision of David's kingdom. Apparently the catastrophes of Israel required more than a political Messiah. They required the unmediated intervention of God himself. Eschatological hope in the Old Testament is not necessarily messianic.

However, the idea of an eschatological Messiah arose mainly in Jewish apocalyptic groups. It was the spiritualization of the messianic hope. How did this happen?

Rabbi Michael Lerner writes, "The tendency to spiritualize reality became increasingly powerful as Jews became increasingly powerless" (Lerner 1994:138). He is referring to the Jews in Judea who were suffering under Greek rule in the second century B.C. when Antiochus IV Epiphanies (175-164 B.C.) was desecrating the temple and burning the Torah (1 Maccabees 1:10-64). Judaism was outlawed, Jews were not allowed to keep the Sabbath, worship in the temple, circumcise their children, or obey the Torah. How should they respond to such oppression? "But many in Israel stood firm and were resolved in their hearts not to eat unclean food. They chose to die rather than to be defiled by food or to profane the holy covenant; and they did die" (1 Macc 1:62-63). Martyrdom.

Another response was *accommodation*. This was the route of the Jewish aristocracy interested in maintaining the status quo and who sought compromise with the foreign powers. Some Jews, however, opted for armed resistance against the Greeks.

This was the reaction of the militants (the Maccabees). Yet another response was "the spiritualizers," those who gave up on human solutions and looked to God alone for miraculous deliverance from on high. It is from this group that apocalyptic literature emerged, such as the book of Daniel, written around 165 B.C. Daniel never mentions the word "messiah," yet the entire book is a dramatic portrayal of the coming messianic age against all odds. For Daniel, God is the one who redeems, and God is the one who intervenes supernaturally to liberate his people. Despite oppression and martyrdom, God is in charge of history and in the last days God will set up his kingdom on earth through an intermediary called "the son of man":

> I saw one like a son of man coming with the clouds of heaven. And he came to the Ancient One and was presented before him. To him was given dominion and glory and kingship, that all peoples, nations, and languages should serve him. His dominion is an everlasting dominion that shall not pass away, and his kingship is one that shall never be destroyed. (Dan 7:13-14)

These words describe the rule of a divinely-appointed eschatological savior. Some have applied these verses to Israel itself, yet over time these verses were interpreted as messianic. The apocalyptic background of this passage points to a redeemer of the end-times whose salvation is universal and transcendent, far exceeding historical Israel. Daniel's "son of man" echoes Isaiah:

> The spirit of the Lord shall rest upon him, the spirit of wisdom and understanding, the spirit of counsel and might, the spirit of knowledge and fear of the Lord . . . with righteousness he shall judge the poor, and decide with equity for the meek of the earth . . . They will not hurt or destroy on all my holy mountain; for the earth will be full of the

knowledge of the Lord as the waters cover the sea. (Isa 11:2-9)

We see that messianic hope in Judaism shifted from the politics of nationalism and hope in a historical messiah (Son of David) to transcendent salvation and hope in an eschatological Messiah (Son of Man). The Messiah became for many Jews a savior for the end-times, a transcendent redeemer. Christianity arose in this religious context. When the Gospels refer to "the Son of Man," they are using an image from Jewish apocalyptic and are describing a universal savior not only for Israel but for the nations.

Contemporary Judaism and the Messiah

> *For the modern Jew, the messianic dream has been transformed and lives on in ways that are greatly different from the traditional belief.*
>
> *--David S. Ariel*

Messianic hope fluctuates between sober realism and idealism. In Judaism, the two sides of messianic hope are *political* and *eschatological.* These are in tension with each other and balance one another. A political Messiah is particular, nationalistic, temporal, and focused exclusively on Israel and God's promises to his people. An eschatological Messiah is universal, transcendent, eternal, cosmic, and focused not only on Israel but also the nations. Hope in the eschatological Messiah is at times expressed in apocalyptic images as contrasted with the Son of David.

Perhaps both aspects are necessary. Politics should not be allowed to swallow up eschatology, and eschatology must always remain grounded in history. The politics of messianism needs the apocalyptic horizon in order to maintain a transcendent dimension. After all, the world is much bigger than literal Israel, and God's plans include a New Creation. Yet the apocalyptic vision can become too transcendent and otherworldly; it needs to stay true to its roots in God's promises to Israel and God's action in history. Furthermore, humans too have a role to play in bringing about the messianic age. We see these tensions played out in contemporary Judaism.

Jews have not ceased reflecting on the Messiah. It is more a matter of emphasis, depending on the theology of a particular movement within Judaism. For many orthodox Jews, the paradigm of Maimonides is still powerful: *an ideal king of the lineage of David who presides over a literal Israel.* This is the political Messiah. Today we would call this a theocracy; it is closely aligned with religious Zionism. There are extreme religious messianists in Israel who envision a literal third temple built on the Temple Mount and who are preparing vestments and utensils for conducting worship and priestly sacrifices.

Moderate to liberal Jews shy away from messianic dreams or visions of a literal temple. They embrace the concept of *tikkun olam.* This Hebrew phrase means "the repairing of the world." What does this include? The most important virtue is responsibility. *Tikkun olam* includes taking personal responsibility for realizing God's kingdom on earth here and now. The call is to work to make the world more just, more humane, and to increase freedom for all people. Messianic deeds are those deeds by which Jews bring about a more just social order. At its heart, Judaism has a revolutionary message for the world: liberation from all structures of domination that oppose God's rule and oppress human beings.

Can we do anything to hasten the coming of the messianic age? Many rabbis have taught that faithful obedience to the Torah will hasten the coming of the Messiah: when Israel at last obeys the Torah, then the Messiah will come. Others believe that the coming of the Messiah must be preceded by disasters or "birth pangs." That is, "when the wickedness of the world has reached its peak, when the 'messianic woes' have come" (Jenni 1962:364).

Certain radical Jewish fundamentalists are willing to force the issue by the use of violence. In 1984, a group of radical Jews were apprehended for planning to blow up the Dome of the Rock in Jerusalem. They believed that such an act would purge the holy precincts from Muslim contamination and pave the way for the coming of the Messiah (Aran 1991). This is a dangerous brand of political messianism that could have disastrous results for the Middle East and the world. More moderate Jews teach that we ourselves bring about the messianic age by making the world a better place for all people. Ariel writes, "Jews believe that the work of creating a perfect world is more important than the Messiah" (Ariel 1995:246).

To summarize, messianism is rooted in the belief that history is moving toward a definite outcome: *God's future.* Messianic hope is always eschatological, but eschatology is not always messianic. God's future can be envisioned without the Messiah in the picture. This future will be either a return to Paradise or an ideal Davidic kingdom centered in Jerusalem, or an earthly utopia brought about by human effort and responsibility. According to apocalyptic writers, history will conclude with a cataclysmic firestorm and the arrival of the Messiah from on high. Thus, hope in the Messiah fluctuates between human responsibility and supernatural intervention.

Despite variations of messianic hope, Jurgen Moltmann comments, "The messianic hope was never the hope of the victors and the rulers. It was always the hope of the defeated and the ground down. The hope of the poor is nothing other than the messianic hope" (Moltmann 1990:13). In the first century A.D., many Jews living on messianic hope felt defeated, ground down, and were poor. They came to believe that Jesus of Nazareth was the long-expected Messiah. The forerunner of the Jesus group was John the Baptist.

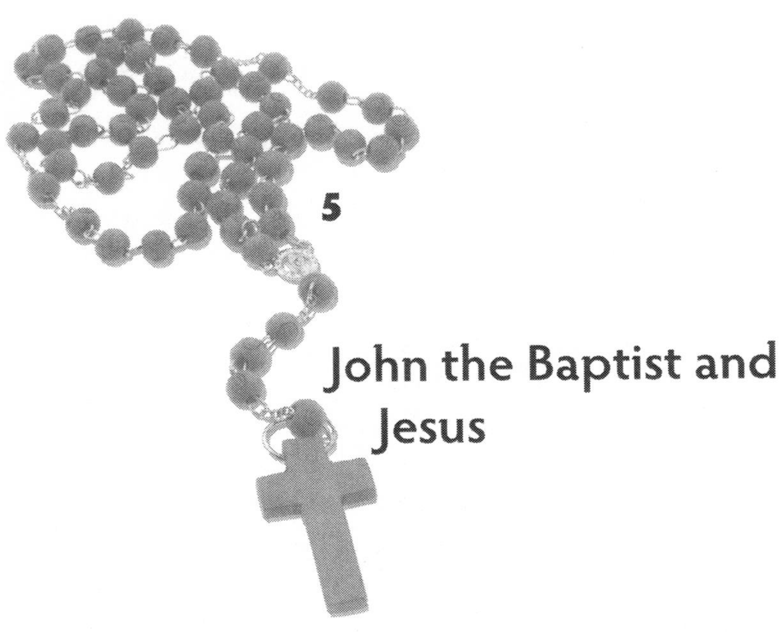

5

John the Baptist and Jesus

John's cruel end was the hour of Jesus' public beginning.

--Jurgen Moltmann

Up to this point we have seen that Jewish apocalyptic is the child of hard times. When God's people are persecuted and oppressed, apocalyptic prophets gain traction. This was true of John the Baptist. John was a remarkable prophet who arose in Israel in the fifteenth year of the reign of the Roman Emperor Tiberias (28-29 A.D.).

John appears suddenly and from out of nowhere, like Elijah. He speaks the word of God to Israel: Israel in waiting, Israel stuck between the past and the future, Israel oppressed by foreign powers, Israel grinding out its existence from day to day, hoping for a miracle, Israel the unprepared and unrepentant people of God. John appears at a time of heightened apocalyptic hopes about the end-times. The wilderness is his home. His message reflects the stark, brutal reality of the barren regions. No frills, no luxury, no equivocating, and nothing to exploit or possess. There is nothing in the wilderness but the word of God.

John avoids Jerusalem, the temple, the worship and rituals, and the elites. He makes no forays into inhabited areas. The people go out to hear him. In the power of the Holy Spirit, he preaches a baptism of repentance for the forgiveness of sins. It is a fork in the road. People must choose to accept or reject him. There is no middle ground, no long and tedious theological hair-splitting, and no complicated exegesis of ancient texts or rabbinic embellishments on oral tradition. "Prepare for the Lord! Get ready now! Repent! There isn't much time left! The kingdom is dawning and God's Messiah is on his way!"

Israel had not seen a prophet like this for centuries. John's baptism was an eschatological sacrament preparing people for the coming messianic age. His life and mission mark both an end and a beginning in salvation history. There is now no going back to religion as usual. Divine salvation is for those who say yes, divine judgment is for those who say no. For when the Coming One arrives, he will clean house and set things right, and it won't be long.

Many Jews reasoned, "But aren't we the chosen people? Isn't Abraham our father? Aren't we wrapped in the secure robe of our divine election and our impeccable spiritual pedigree?" No, John proclaimed. Unconditional election for the nation was a myth. Election could not save Israel from the wrath to come. God's chosen people and literal Israel are not identical. God cannot be held hostage by a presumptuous faith. Repent or else!

John's ministry was brief. Such urgency can't be sustained for years on end. John expected a quick resolution. John shouted the coming judgment of God. How long does a shout last? Not very long, but a shout echoes, and Judaism at that time was an echo chamber of apocalyptic and revolutionary voices crying out for change, for salvation, and for the Messiah. John's echo must have reached Galilee, for Jesus came from Galilee in the north to be baptized by John. He must have been struck by John's apocalyptic message. Jesus identified himself with John's movement and placed himself squarely on the side of apocalyptic fervor.

John suffered a tragic fate: beheaded by Herod Antipas. Later, Jesus would suffer a tragic fate: crucified on a Roman cross. Regarding John, Jesus said, "Truly I tell you, among those born of women no one has arisen greater than John the Baptist . . . For all the prophets and the law prophesied until John came; and if you are willing to accept it, he is Elijah who is to come" (Matt 11:11, 13-14).

Elijah Who Is To Come

But I tell you that Elijah has come, and they did to him whatever they pleased, as it is written about him.
--Mark 9:13

There was a strand of Jewish eschatology that believed God would send another Elijah to prepare his people for the Messiah. Elijah will return to usher in the end-times. Christian faith views John the Baptist as this "Elijah who is to come." The stories about John in the New Testament are entirely shaped by Christian faith. John the Baptist is important to Christians solely because of his relationship to Jesus.

First, we will explore the Jewish hope for a coming Elijah who will prepare the way for the Messiah.

Ben Sira was a Jewish teacher in Jerusalem from about 200-180 B.C. At that time, Judea was a war zone torn apart by a power struggle between the Ptolemaic and Seleucid dynasties. Palestine was an occupied territory and the Jews chafed under foreign domination. In his collection of teachings, Ben Sira wrote,

> How glorious you were, Elijah, in your wondrous deeds!
> Whose glory is equal to yours? . . . At the appointed time, it is written, you are destined to calm the wrath of God before it breaks out in fury, to turn the hearts of the parents to their children, and to restore the tribes of Jacob. (Sirach 48:4,10)

Restoration for the tribes of Jacob! Elijah appearing! Ben Sira summarizes the hope of Jews for liberation and the coming of Elijah the prophet to usher in the messianic age.

The key text, however, is found in the last book of the Old Testament:

> Lo, I will send you the prophet Elijah before the great and terrible day of the Lord comes. He will turn the hearts of the parents to their children and the hearts of the children to their parents, so that I will not come and strike the land with a curse. (Malachi 4:5-6)

Malachi means "messenger." This messenger viewed the day of the Lord as a day of judgment upon Israel. The Coming One would be like "a refiner's fire" and would "purify the descendents of Levi" (Mal 3:1-4). John the Baptist was familiar with these texts and modeled his ministry accordingly. John announced the soon-coming judgment of God as a day of wrath. It could be described as the birth pangs of the messianic age.

Another important text is Isaiah 40:3-5, which elaborates on the wilderness theme:

> A voice cries out: "In the wilderness prepare the way of the Lord, make straight in the desert a highway for our God. Every valley shall be lifted up, and every mountain and hill be made low; the uneven ground shall become level, and the rough places a plane. Then the glory of the Lord shall be revealed . . ."

John appeared in the wilderness as an ascetic misfit dressed like Elijah the prophet and working in the region where Elijah had hidden out centuries before. Joseph Klausner writes, "Since he did not eat bread nor drink wine he was regarded by the ordinary people as a holy man; but the Pharisees and Scribes, and the educated classes generally, thought him mad" (Klausner 1964:245). This concurs with what Jesus said, "John came neither eating nor drinking, and they say, 'He as a demon'" (Matt 11:18). The religious authorities and aristocracy rejected John. When Sadducees and Pharisees came to John from Jerusalem he called them snakes:

> You brood of vipers! Who warned you to flee from the wrath to come? Bear fruit worthy of repentance. Do not presume to say to yourselves, "We have Abraham as our ancestor"; for I tell you, God is able from these stones to raise up children to Abraham. Even now the ax is lying at the root of the trees . . ." (Matt 3:7-10)

Here John is not only criticizing the hypocrisy of the Jewish leaders; he is cutting them out of the kingdom of God, cutting them out of God's elect people. Though John preaches to the nation Israel, he is not baptizing a nation. He is baptizing individual Jews who repent, change their ways, and then reenter Judea and Galilee like "ticking time bombs" loaded with apocalyptic expectations (Crossan 1994:43). They constitute a new Israel, a faithful remnant in the midst of a complacent and prideful nation. John the Baptist redefined election. He harkened back to the old "remnant theology" of the prophets: only a remnant will be saved, but the nation as a whole is wicked and under God's judgment. Jesus carried on this message in his conflict with the scribes and Pharisees. This message is based on a new understanding of election. Literal descent from Abraham means nothing. Only repentance and conversion prepare one for the coming Messiah.

But the common people—the peasants—listened to John and were baptized. In fact, Herod Antipas feared the crowd because they regarded John as a prophet (Matt 14:5). The chief priests and elders also feared the crowd for the same reason (Matt 21:26). John created a populist movement among those outside the power structures. These included those "outside the law," those who did not keep the Torah properly and who were despised by the pious religionists. Luke mentions this rabble composed of "the crowds" and tax collectors and even soldiers. Soldiers, too? According to Luke, John the Baptist spoke the word of God to the rejected, to sinners, to outcasts, and to Roman soldiers (Lk 3:10-14). Again, we find a preview of things to come in the ministry of Jesus. Not only does Jesus redefine election, he aims his message at sinners who have been written off by the religious establishment.

John Dominic Crossan views John's ministry as "peasant apocalypticism" (Crossan 1994:40). John left no literary trail. He never wrote an apocalyptic drama like Daniel or Revelation. John was not a part of any apocalyptic literary circle. Yet John was similar to other apocalyptic prophets that appeared in Judea and Galilee from the thirties through the sixties A.D. Crossan writes, "Apocalyptic prophets led large crowds into the wilderness so that they could recross the Jordan into the Promised Land, which God would then restore to them as of old under Moses and Joshua" (Crossan 1994:42). There is a typology going on in John's baptism. He is reenacting the Exodus, the wilderness wanderings, the crossing of the Jordan River, and entry into Canaan. The main trait of the apocalyptic viewpoint is rescue from God alone. Once God's people have purified themselves, God will act to destroy his enemies and set up his righteous kingdom. It is transcendental hope. Human effort to bring about the kingdom is futile. God alone can intervene with judgment and salvation. The common people found hope in this message, but the ruling elites were threatened by it.

John's message was a challenge to both religious and political power. It was grounded in the power of the Spirit, for we are told that John was filled with the Holy Spirit "even before his birth" (Lk 1:15). This does not imply that John was conceived by the power of the Spirit but that he was destined by God from birth to carry out a special mission, "to make ready a people prepared for the Lord" (Lk 1:17). John confronted power like Elijah confronted King Ahab and Jezebel. John was also recapitulating the actions of Moses and

Joshua in the wilderness, crossing the Jordan, and entering the Promised Land.

Why was Jesus Baptized?

In those days Jesus came from Nazareth in Galilee and was baptized by John in the Jordan.

--Mark 1:9

But why was Jesus baptized by John?

The baptism of Jesus can be viewed as an embarrassment, that is, "the superior one" submitting to "the inferior one." Matthew addresses this problem by emphasizing John's unwillingness to baptize Jesus: "I need to be baptized by you, and do you come to me?" Jesus answered, "Let it be so now; for it is proper for us in this way to fulfill all righteousness." John then consents to baptize Jesus (Matt 3:13-15). As Gunther Bornkamm remarks, "It is clear that Christian reflection is expressed in these verses, passed on only by Matthew, which looks back in faith on the person and life of Jesus as a whole" (Bornkamm 1960:48). We should not interpret Jesus' baptism as an act of modesty or just going through the motions. Jesus was not playing a game, nor was he a sinner needing to be converted. Rather, the baptism of Jesus was the endpoint of John's mission. It was a divine "must" in order for Jesus to be anointed with the Spirit and inaugurate the messianic age.

The Gospels agree that Jesus emerged from John's movement and that John's baptism was the foundation of Jesus' mission (Moltmann 1993:87). Did Jesus remain part of John's movement? All we know is that the arrest of John was a turning point for Jesus. It marked the moment when Jesus officially began his public ministry. Second, Crossan speculates that John's fate might have caused Jesus to rethink the apocalyptic approach to things. Perhaps God did not operate through apocalyptic fireworks. Crossan observes, "The major question is not whether Jesus *began* as an apocalyptic believer but whether he *continued* as such and whether, when he began his own mission, he did so by picking up the fallen banner of the Baptist" (Crossan 1994:46). We must linger a moment on this question, for it raises the issue of *dissimilarities* between John and Jesus.

John the Baptist and Jesus shared a common dedication to God and to God's cause. They agreed that they were living at a key time in Israel's history and that God was about to do a mighty thing. They agreed that the kingdom was drawing near and people needed to repent. But they differed in their style, their mission, and their message.

At his baptism, Jesus was endowed with the Holy Spirit from on high and declared to be the Son of God: "This is my Son, the Beloved, with whom I am well pleased" (Matt 3:17). This anointing by the Spirit and the declaration of sonship set Jesus apart from all others and was the basis for his messianic mission. It was his call. Just as the king of Israel was anointed by the Spirit and declared to be a "son" of God (Ps 2:7), Jesus received his messianic anointing and, from that point on, John fades into the background. Jesus was driven into the desert following his baptism. His forty days in the wilderness clarified his mission as *a suffering Messiah*, a Messiah who would not exploit power to achieve earthly, political ends.

Furthermore, John was an ascetic who lived apart from society; Jesus ate and drank with tax collectors and sinners and Pharisees, and focused his ministry on the busy villages of Galilee. There is nothing ascetic or monkish about Jesus. John preached the coming wrath of God; Jesus preached the joy of entering into the kingdom of God and the marvelous grace of God toward the poor, the sick, the lame, and the outcasts. But in the end, the main difference between John the Baptist and Jesus is the difference between *promise and fulfillment*. John represents the promise of the age to come; Jesus fulfills it. John points forward to the messianic age; Jesus brings in the messianic age. John is the messenger; Jesus is the embodiment of the message. John is the forerunner; Jesus is the Messiah.

Did John the Baptist misinterpret Jesus? It appears that he did. Jesus did not turn out to be the instrument of God's wrath that John had predicted. Jesus did not arrive with "a winnowing fork in his hand" in order to carry out God's final and fiery judgment. Jesus was an enigma to John, and perhaps a disappointment. While in prison, John sent messengers to Jesus to ask him, "Are you the one who is to come, or are we to wait for another?" (Matt 11:3). This text shows the division between John and his disciples, and Jesus and his disciples. By that time, they were separate movements on separate tracks with separate agendas. Apparently, Jesus was not living up to John's apocalyptic expectations of the Messiah. Where is the judgment? Where is the kingdom? Where are political liberation and the New Age? Jesus' answer is a statement about his vision of the kingdom: his mission is more prophetic than apocalyptic. He says,

> Go and tell John what you hear and see: the blind receive their sight, the lame walk, the lepers are cleansed, the deaf hear, the dead are raised, and the poor have good news brought to them. And blessed is anyone who takes no offense at me. (Matt 11:4-6)

These are certainly not apocalyptic deeds! But as far as Jesus is concerned, they are messianic signs of the presence of the kingdom of God. They fulfill the promise of the prophets of old. Here is a clear indication that Jesus identified himself more closely with the *prophetic* tradition of Israel than with the *apocalyptic* tradition (see Chapter Six). John the Baptist was expecting an apocalyptic savior; Jesus was a Messiah who functioned as a prophet, a healer, a teacher, and a suffering servant who eventually would be crucified.

Prior to this, John's disciples confronted Jesus about fasting (Matt 9:14-17). Jesus' disciples did not fast as a sign of penitence.

The messianic banquet had already begun and the present age of God's kingdom should be celebrated, like a wedding feast. There is no glum fasting in preparation for the end times. No more strident spiritual disciplines for penitence. Jesus the Messiah brings the kingdom, and the powers of the kingdom are here now. New wine has replaced old wine. Fresh wineskins are needed for this new messianic wine. John's disciples represent "old wine" and "old wineskins." The rivalry between John's disciples and Jesus' disciples continued for years. The Apostle Paul, years later, encountered a group of John's disciples in Ephesus (Acts19:1-7).

All the law and the prophets prophesied until John came; since John, the kingdom of God has arrived and has met with violent resistance and controversy (Matt 11:11-15). This is how Jesus viewed things. John was the greatest prophet who ever lived because he was the forerunner of the Messiah. Nevertheless, John remains on the "promise" side of eschatology, not the "fulfillment" side. This is why whoever is least in the kingdom of God is greater than John (Matt 11:11). John's mission was over. "It is not enough to await a future kingdom; one must enter a present one here and now" (Crossan 1994:48).

John the Baptist represents waiting for the coming apocalyptic kingdom as a repentant sinner. Jesus, on the other hand, brings in the messianic age of grace, hope, and good news for the poor, the oppressed, and the outcasts.

Conclusion

He must increase, but I must decrease.

--John 3:30

John the Baptist is now a figure from the past. But spiritually, John belongs to the proclamation of the church. He has become "St. John the Baptist"! Each Advent season Christians read about him. Whenever the church celebrates the baptism of Jesus, John is mentioned. Yet John the Baptist is not the heart of Christian faith. John did not follow Jesus. John remains a solitary, transitional figure, a bridge between two ages. Once Jesus arrives, John fades from the scene. Mission accomplished.

While John was certainly not a Christian, we can place him squarely in the tradition of Jewish apocalyptic prophets. Jesus did not pick up the fallen banner of John. He left it lying there and went on with his own messianic preaching and teaching. A new age arrived in Jesus, and this age did not have the apocalyptic fireworks that John expected. Jesus not only preached the nearness of the kingdom of God, he embodied the arrival of the kingdom here and now. Thus, for the church John the Baptist can be only a transitional figure. Nevertheless, he is "Elijah," the greatest of the prophets who pointed the way to the coming God.

6

Did Jesus Believe in the End of the World?

Do not be afraid, little flock, for it is your Father's good pleasure to give you the kingdom.

--Luke 12:32

This chapter is about Jesus and the end of the world. Did Jesus believe in the end of the world? If so, what did he mean by this? Did Jesus believe in the Rapture, Armageddon, Antichrist—the whole apocalyptic package?

Our focus is on Jesus as an eschatological prophet of the last days, announcing the coming of God's kingdom. He believed the kingdom was already breaking in and would soon arrive in its fullness and power. He believed in the coming of "the Son of Man," a transcendent hero from on high, sent to rescue God's people and destroy God's enemies. To a certain degree, Jesus was under the spell of Jewish apocalyptic.

The first followers of Jesus did not adopt the apocalyptic mindset out of nowhere. The apocalyptic worldview of the early church goes back to Jesus himself. At the beginning of his public ministry, Jesus associated himself with John the Baptist, an apocalyptic prophet. Jesus' life was framed by an apocalyptic prophet at the beginning and an apocalyptic church at the end. It seems only reasonable to see an apocalyptic Jesus in the middle (Ehrman 2000).

Jesus announced "the time is fulfilled" (Mk 1:15). He lived in intense expectation of the advent of God's kingdom. He expected something amazing to happen in the near future. In light of God's approaching future, people must repent and get ready now. There must be a new way of living, a new attitude, a new mental outlook, and radical conversion. The ethics of Jesus are preparation for the coming kingdom of God (see Chapter Eight).

Thus, the present and future are interwoven in Jesus and cannot be separated. The kingdom is here now, yet the kingdom is arriving soon. God's lordship can be seen, felt, and experienced now, yet God is about to act in a dramatic way to set up his final rule. This is the dialectic between present and future or "Already/Not Yet."

The Reign of God is Beginning Now!

If it is by the finger of God that I cast out demons, then the kingdom of God has come to you.

--Luke 11:20

Jesus cast out demons. He was doing more than impressing people with his powers. He was invading Satan's territory and taking over. He was engaged in a spiritual battle with evil, attacking Satan's reign with the powers of God's reign, as we see in the following verses,

- If it is by the finger of God that I cast out demons, then the kingdom of God has come to you. (Lk 11:20)
- I watched Satan fall from heaven like a flash of lightning. (Lk 10:18)
- No one can enter a strong man's house and plunder his

> property without first tying up the strong man; then indeed the house can be plundered. (Mk 3:27)

Through his exorcisms and healings, Jesus was plundering Satan's property. He was taking back what belongs to God and reclaiming God's rightful territory. Even now the demons are screaming out. Even now the demons are losing ground. Even now the demons are begging Jesus not to send them "back into the abyss" (Lk 5:31). The demons cry out, "What have you to do with us, Jesus of Nazareth? Have you come to destroy us?" (Mk 1:24). Satan's time has expired and his kingdom is collapsing (Bultmann 1951, 1:5-6). This is the liberation of God. God liberates those who are oppressed by Satan, and this liberation is taking place not in some distant, apocalyptic future, but *now.*

Why search the sky for signs and wonders? Why spend time trying to interpret cryptic prophecies found in apocalyptic books? According to Jesus, the signs are present here and now,

- You know how to interpret the appearance of earth and sky, but why do you not know how to interpret the present time? (Lk 12:56)
- The kingdom of God is not coming with calculations and things that can be observed; nor will they say, 'Look, here it is!' or 'There it is!' For, in fact, the kingdom of God is in your midst! (Lk 17:20-21)
- Blessed are the eyes that see what you see! For I tell you that many prophets and kings desired to see what you see, but did not see it, and to hear what you hear, but did not hear it. (Lk 10:23-24)
- The blind receive their sight, the lame walk, the lepers are cleansed, the deaf hear, the dead are raised, and the poor have good news brought to them. (Matt 11:5)
- The time is fulfilled and the kingdom of God has come near; repent, and believe in the good news. (Mk 1:15)

God's reign is beginning now. Jesus is referring to the arrival of the age of salvation, the great messianic age foretold by the prophets. The deeds of the messianic age are now erupting in the midst of this present evil age. This is happening in the person of Jesus himself. Gunther Bornkamm writes, "God's victory over Satan takes place in his words and deeds, and it is in them that the signs of this victory are erected" (Bornkamm 1960:68).

Unlike apocalyptic seers, Jesus offers no detailed, play-by-play information about the future. He does not dabble in calculations about the end of the world or construct futuristic fantasies. He has one message: "God will reign, and God's reign is beginning now! You must choose!" Everyone encountering Jesus was faced with a decision. Wherever he went, there was an ending and a beginning, a moment of truth: to follow or not to follow, to surrender to the reign of God or to resist.

Moreover, Jesus rejected the old nationalistic hopes of Israel. He has nothing to say about overthrowing the Romans and establishing the ideal Davidic kingdom. He left those fantasies behind. No zealous nationalism, no violent revolt, no hyper-patriotism, no pious law-keeping to hasten the coming of the Messiah. Rather, Jesus called for a decision now in regard to the reign of God that is beginning now with his ministry and message.

Jesus stressed that people should make the kingdom their top priority. They should value the kingdom like a man who finds a treasure in a field and sells everything to buy the field, or like a merchant who discovers a great pearl and sells everything to purchase it (Matt 13:44-46). Consider these words,

- Strive first for the kingdom of God and his righteousness, and all these things will be given to you as well. (Matt 6:33)
- No one can serve two masters . . . You cannot serve God and wealth. (Matt 6:24)
- Sell your possessions and do works of charity. Make purses for yourselves that do not wear out, an unfailing treasure in heaven, where no thief comes near and no moth destroys.

For where your treasure is, there your heart will be also. (Lk 12:33-34)

People came and listened, and were healed and liberated and given hope. Others came and doubted and criticized. But in each case, something ended and something began. Each person went one way or the other in regard to Jesus and the reign of God.

Jesus brought division. He said,

- I came to bring fire to the earth, and how I wish it were already kindled! I have a baptism with which to be baptized, and what stress I am under until it is completed! Do you think that I have come to bring peace to the earth? No, I tell you, but rather division! (Lk 12:49-51)
- Do not think that I have come to bring peace to the earth; I have not come to bring peace, but a sword. (Matt 10:34)

Families were torn down the middle and lives were uprooted, such as the lives of his disciples: "They left everything and followed him" (Lk 5:11). Jesus renounced his own family in order to carry out his mission with unwavering single-mindedness: "And looking at those who sat around him, he said, 'Here are my mother and my brothers! Whoever does the will of God is my brother and sister and mother" (Mk 3:34-35).

Those who are preoccupied with worldly affairs cannot enter God's reign. So, the message goes out to the highways and byways, and "the poor, the crippled, the blind, and the lame" respond (Lk 14:15-24). Those who cannot part with their wealth are passed by: "How hard it will be for those who have wealth to enter the kingdom of God!" (Mk 10:23). Those who are called to follow Jesus as disciples are not given time to finish up family obligations: "Let the dead bury their own dead; but as for you, go and proclaim the kingdom of God" (Lk 9:60). To say no to Jesus and his message about the reign of God is to say no to God himself and to misinterpret the times.

The message of the kingdom is like new wine that must be poured into new wineskins; yet many prefer the old wine, saying, "The old is good enough" (Lk 5:37-39). But God is doing something new! God has hidden the truth of the kingdom from "the wise and the intelligent" and revealed it to "infants" (Lk 10:21). One must become "as a little child" to enter the kingdom (Lk 18:17). Jesus speaks with astounding authority, unlike the scribes and Pharisees (Mk 1:22, 27; Matt 7:28-29).

To Jesus, the present moment is the last hour before "the end."

Jesus pressed on despite resistance from the Jewish authorities. His focus was "the lost sheep of the house of Israel" (Matt 10:6). This was the worn out flock without a shepherd (Matt 9:36). It does not appear that Jesus carried out an intentional mission to the Gentiles. He maintained that "salvation is from the Jews," meaning the reign of God is still mediated to the world via Israel (Jn 4:22). Yet Jesus did not ignore Gentiles. Non-Jews came to him and recognized God's actions in him (Jn 12:20-21). A Roman Centurion came and believed. Jesus said, "Truly I tell you, in no one in Israel have I found such faith" (Matt 8:10). A woman of Samaria believed Jesus was the Messiah (Jn 4:7-42). A Samaritan leper whom Jesus healed returned to praise God and give thanks (Lk 17:11-19). The faith of a woman from Tyre (Gentile territory) was rewarded by Jesus when he cured her daughter's illness (Mk 7:24-30).

Jesus emphasized that "the last will be first, and the first will be last" (Matt 20:16). There would be many surprises in the kingdom of God! For example,

> I tell you, many will come from east and west and will eat with Abraham and Isaac and Jacob in the kingdom of heaven, while the heirs of the kingdom will be thrown into the outer darkness, where there will be weeping and gnashing of teeth. (Matt 8:11-12)

Jesus focused on the importance of the present moment as a time of decision. God was immediately present, summoning people to decide for or against the kingdom. That kingdom was present *now.* Already the kingdom was breaking into world history in the person of Jesus: the presence of the kingdom of God in the Christ.

And yet . . . it was coming soon. Here we are faced with the tension of New Testament eschatology: *already present, yet on its way.* We now turn to the kingdom as a future event.

The Reign of God is Coming Soon!

> *Your kingdom come, your will be done on earth, as it is in heaven.*
>
> --*Matthew* 6:10

Jesus prayed, "Your kingdom come, your will be done on earth as it is in heaven." These are apocalyptic words rooted in apocalyptic hopes. When praying these words, we are praying for the end of the world.

The petition, "Lead us not into temptation, but deliver us from evil," refers to the time of tribulation at the end of time. A better translation is, "Save us from the apocalyptic time of trouble, and deliver us from the Evil One." This is a prayer for deliverance from the end-time catastrophe that is coming upon the world.

Jesus prayed for the coming of God's reign on earth. He expected the imminent arrival of God's universal kingdom on earth. He lived with an intense expectation that God would soon act to set up his rule on earth. Jesus drew on images from Daniel. Consider these words regarding "the Son of Man":

- For the Son of Man is to come with his angels in the glory of his Father, and then he will repay everyone for what has been done. Truly I tell you, there are some standing here who will not taste death before they see the Son of Man coming in his kingdom. (Matt 16:27-28)

- Then they will see the Son of Man coming in clouds with great power and glory. Then he will send out his angels, and gather his elect from the four winds, from the ends of the earth to the ends of heaven. (Mk 13:26-27)
- The Son of Man will send his angels, and they will collect out of his kingdom all causes of sin and all evildoers, and they will throw them into the furnace of fire, where there will be weeping and gnashing of teeth. (Matt 13:41-42)
- Therefore you must also be ready, for the Son of Man is coming at an unexpected hour. (Matt 24:44)

Jesus, it seems, expected a supernatural intervention by God through a transcendent figure called "the Son of Man." He announced the imminent advent of God's kingdom in power mediated by the Son of Man, the eschatological judge of the end-times. Daniel 7:13-14 reads,

> I saw one like a son of man coming with the clouds of heaven. And he came to the Ancient One and was presented before him. To him was given dominion and glory and kingship, that all the peoples, nations, and languages should serve him. His dominion is an everlasting dominion that shall not pass away, and his kingdom is one that shall never be destroyed.

The Son of Man is the eschatological judge who establishes God's reign on earth at the end of time. Jesus did not expect time to drag on indefinitely,

- I tell you, you will not have gone through all the towns of Israel before the Son of Man comes. (Matt 10:23)
- Truly I tell you, this generation will not pass away until all these things have taken place. (Matt 24:34)

Hans Kung notes, "There is not a single saying of Jesus which postpones the end-event to the distant future" (Kung 1976:216). Jesus expected the end of the world *in his lifetime*. In so doing, he was reflecting the apocalyptic mood of his generation.

Yet Jesus never obsessed about signs and wonders. He never set dates for the end or dabbled in apocalyptic calculations: "But about that day and hour no one knows, neither the angels of heaven, nor the Son, but only the Father" (Matt 24:36). Jesus never formed an ascetic commune and moved out to the desert to wait for deliverance from on high. Jesus' belief in the imminent end did not lead him to reject the world or to become a pessimist. Rather, the coming kingdom is good news,

- Blessed are the meek, for they will inherit the earth. (Matt 5:5)
- Do not be afraid, little flock, for it is your Father's good pleasure to give you the kingdom. (Lk 12:32)
- Truly I tell you, at the renewal of all things, when the Son of Man is seated on the throne of his glory, you who have followed me will also sit on twelve thrones, judging the twelve tribes of Israel. (Matt 19:28)

Despite his belief in the coming judgment of the world, Jesus' message was positive and hopeful. The love, mercy, and compassion of God for all people are being experienced now. Even now the poor, the sick, the blind, and the lame are rejoicing. Sinners are being forgiven and saved. The outcasts are coming in. The lost are found, like sheep, like coins, like the prodigal son (Lk 15).

The trend of Judaism at that time was toward sectarian exclusiveness, but Jesus announced universal acceptance. He formed no holy remnant. If he divided the people at all, it was between those who repent and those who don't. Everyone has a choice. God's lordship is for all, just as God's love is for all. There is no sectarian arrogance here, but rather a positive message to those who have ears to hear and hearts to accept it (Schillebeeckx 1979:144-145).

But woe to those who don't accept it. For them, the coming kingdom will be judgment, not salvation. "There will be weeping and gnashing of teeth." The end is near. If the end is near, people must get ready and be prepared. Jesus says,

- Be dressed for action and have your lamps lit . . . for the Son of Man is coming at an unexpected hour . . . Beware, keep alert; for you do not know when the time will come . . . And what I say to you, I say to all: Keep awake!" (Mk 13:33, 37)

"Jesus did not want to provide information about the end of time, but to issue a call for the present in view of the approaching end" (Kung 1976:222).

The apocalyptic vision of Jesus shaped his attitude toward the temple in Jerusalem. Jesus predicted the destruction of the temple as part of his end-time scenario. The temple was the heart of Jewish faith and the central symbol of Judaism. The temple was the holiest place in the world for Jews, the dwelling place of God himself. Yet Jesus cleansed the temple during the final week of his life (Matt 21:12-17; Mk 11:15-19; Lk 19:45-48). This event led to his condemnation by the Jewish authorities. Why? Was Jesus calling for changes in the way things were done around the temple, or was Jesus forecasting the destruction of the temple itself? After assessing the temple texts, E. P. Sanders favors the latter view: *Jesus cleansed the temple as a sign of the temple's future destruction at the end of time*. The cleansing of the temple was an apocalyptic act based on apocalyptic dogma. Sanders writes,

> He was a prophet, and an eschatological prophet. He thought that God was about to destroy the Temple . . . Jesus probably thought that in the new age, when the twelve tribes of Israel were again assembled, there would be a new and perfect Temple built by God himself. That was standard eschatological or new-age thinking. (Sanders 1993:261)

This issue highlights the apocalyptic mindset of Jesus. Everything Jesus said and did was related to his conviction that the end was coming soon. Time was not going to drag on much longer. God's future was on the way, just around the corner. Not even the temple would survive the coming catastrophe.

We now know that it didn't happen that way. The temple was not destroyed by the Son of Man but by the Romans in 70 A.D.

As his mission progressed, Jesus began to teach "that the Son of Man must undergo great suffering, and be rejected by the elders, and the scribes, and be killed, and after three days rise again" (Mk 8:31). Perhaps his death would force God's hand and bring in the kingdom? We will never know. Albert Schweitzer believed that Jesus forced the issue by going to Jerusalem to provoke a crisis that would bring about the final cataclysm. He writes, "His death was grounded in dogma" (Schweitzer 1998:392). Apocalyptic dogma. Jesus combined the image of the Son of Man with the image of the Suffering Servant from Isaiah 53. The Son of Man must die vicariously in order for the kingdom of God to come in its fullness. Through his death, the kingdom would come. Even the death of Jesus becomes an apocalyptic act or "the apocalyptic sufferings of Christ" (Moltmann 1993:151-159).

I elaborate on the eschatological death of Jesus in a later chapter (see Chapter Nine). But the question arises, "Was Jesus wrong?"

Was Jesus Wrong?

It terms of cosmic knowledge it was an error.

--Hans Kung

We cannot deny the fact that the end did not occur as Jesus predicted. The Son of Man never arrived. The final cataclysm never happened. Regarding his belief in the imminent end of the world, it's hard to deny that Jesus was wrong.

Furthermore, we no longer live in a mythological, apocalyptic universe. Apocalyptic, as I pointed out earlier, is a time-conditioned worldview that becomes absurd if taken literally and used to forecast future events. The apocalyptic hopes of the early church faded as time went on. This shift from imminent expectation to marking time can be seen in the New Testament itself. In the Gospel of John (late first century), the apocalyptic horizon has entirely disappeared (see Chapter Eleven). Christians had to settle down in time and history, acknowledging that they would probably be around a while. Some redefined the concept of time itself, as we read in 2 Peter,

> But do not ignore this one fact, beloved, that with the Lord one day is like a thousand years, and a thousand years are like one day. The Lord is not slow about his promise, as some think of slowness, but is patient with you, not wanting any to perish, but all to come to repentance. (2 Pt 3:8-9)

We are left with the same task as the early church, namely, reinterpreting Jesus for our own time. This means going behind the apocalyptic mindset of Jesus to what is really decisive and abiding. His message is *a warning and a promise leading to responsibility and hope.*

- *Warning:* Do not ignore the present moment. God is here now. Repent and receive God's grace and mercy. You cannot decide for or against God beyond time and history. Change your ways and start living according to God's kingdom.
- *Promise:* It is God's good pleasure to give you the blessings of the kingdom as a free gift. God's future is for all who receive God's love. Today is a new day. The promise is for you, no matter how sinful you are. Do not fear, for God is on your side, and God is gracious, kind, and generous.
- *Responsibility:* Take up your cross and follow Jesus in the way of self-sacrifice and service. Commit yourself to God's cause and let nothing stand in your way. Feed the hungry,

visit the sick and those in prison, forgive and you will be forgiven, be extravagant in showing mercy, lift up the faint-hearted, take a stand for justice, speak out against hypocrisy, freely give as you have freely received, and then die like Jesus. Share his lot.

- *Hope:* God who created all things will bring an end to all things. The future is *God's future.* Therefore, hope! God has not forgotten this world but is bringing all things to a resolution. In the end, hope is openness to God's future.

Jesus' message about the end of the world is *a warning and promise leading to responsibility and hope.* We can affirm these without embracing an apocalyptic worldview. We can affirm a positive and reasonable hope that counters despair, cynicism, indifference, and decadence. This is a hope that results in a certain way of life, in other words, ethics. In the following chapter we will explore the ethics of Jesus and the kingdom of God.

7

Mark 13: Soon, But Not That Soon

And what I say to you I say to all: Keep awake.
--Mark 13:37

The paradox of apocalyptic hope is this:

- The end is always near, but it never happens
- Jesus is coming soon, but not that soon
- The end will happen suddenly, but not very quickly
- Time is short, but no one knows the hour of the end

Meanwhile, the church is in a period of witnessing and waiting. The church is a witnessing church; the church is a waiting church. The church is living a paradox.

Mark 13 is a collection of traditions about the coming of the Son of Man and the end of the age. Here we enter the mythological worldview of early Christian apocalyptic. Mark 13 has been called "the little apocalypse." Jesus is speaking to a few curious disciples, explaining events leading up to the end. It is impossible to know how much of Mark 13 is original with Jesus and how much is the work of a complex editing process. The chapter is a composite of various apocalyptic teachings. Some of these teachings go back to Jesus, some don't.

Mark 13 is written for a messianic and millenarian religious group. This group sees itself as God's elect and expects the end to come soon. Vindication is on the way. Soon the domination systems of this world will be destroyed and God will set up his eternal kingdom. This was the apocalyptic hope of primitive Christianity. Christianity began as a messianic/millenarian sect within Judaism centered on Jesus. Christianity is a religion of expectation.

But we must ask an obvious question, "Why does Mark 13 exist at all?" Primarily because,

- The world did not end, and the Son of Man never arrived in power and glory
- The church had to deal with the passage of time
- Yet the church had to preserve its apocalyptic perspective and future hope

The fact that Mark was written at all proves that Christians at that time were trying to make sense of their place in history precisely because history did not end as expected. Time was beginning to drag on. Nothing challenges apocalyptic hopes more than time dragging on. The longer time goes on, the harder it is to keep hope alive. Once an apocalyptic movement begins writing things down, apocalyptic hope is already beginning to die out.

The church is no longer an apocalyptic community waiting on tiptoe for the coming of the Lord. Yet Mark 13 still confronts us with an important message for Christians today. This is a brief chapter that will focus on Christian expectation about the end, and the nature of the church.

Great Expectations and Repeated Disappointments

Apocalyptic groups are known for great expectations and repeated disappointments. Christian history is littered with predictions about the end, predictions that never came true. These apocalyptic spasms are generated by a sense of discontentment and political powerlessness, and are fueled by the apocalyptic visions of the Bible. Mark 13 is one of those apocalyptic passages.

Mark 13 revolves around *power*. The Son of Man will appear in power and glory. Hostile powers will be conquered by the power of God, and "God's elect" will be saved. The central message of apocalyptic is the final triumph of God over all anti-God powers. God appears in power and glory to rescue his powerless people who are being persecuted. The thrust of apocalyptic hope is always about power. Apocalyptic is the hope of the powerless for a powerful God to save them from hostile powers (see Chapter Two).

If we accept that the Gospel of Mark was written during 65-70 A.D., then we see the fledgling Christian community trying to survive amidst hostile powers, namely, the Roman Empire and Judaism. Christianity at this time was characterized by three features,

- Minority status
- No political power
- Persecution

These features are evident in Mark 13. There is no call to arms, no call to revolt, and no call to change the system. Such activities would have been suicidal. Rather, Christians need to hunker down, wait it out, and hope in the coming of the Son of Man "in power and glory." Only a supernatural rescue from heaven would save them. Meanwhile, they are to bear witness before synagogues, governors, and kings, and be persecuted.

Yet, as John G. Gager points out, "by definition no millenarian cult can long survive in its original form" (Gager 1975:21). Great expectations must eventually come to terms with history. Apocalyptic fervor must eventually be modified. Any religious movement must organize itself and become institutionalized if it is to continue on for centuries. Apocalyptic spasms don't last. Apocalyptic hope is exciting for a while, but one can't build a church on it without a large measure of "cognitive dissonance."

Cognitive dissonance is a sociological term describing "a condition of distress and doubt stemming from the disconfirmation of an important belief" (Gager 1975:39). For example, what happens when a religious group sets a date for the end of the world and the prophecy fails to come true? History disconfirms the prediction and the group has to make sense of what *didn't* happen. Yet the disappointment does not usually result in the group disbanding. The group is likely to intensify its message, increase its proselytizing, and reinterpret the prophecies.

This was the case for the early church. Christianity is two thousand years of cognitive dissonance modified by toning down and reinterpreting its apocalyptic message. The apocalyptic impulse of Jesus and primitive Christianity was tamed. The end did not occur. The Son of Man did not appear. The disappointment, however, did not destroy the Christian community. The message became "Witness and wait, and don't set dates for the end!" In summary,

- The church is called to witness to the gospel and to suffer with Christ
- The church is called to wait and hope
- The church must not set a date for the end

This leads us back to Mark 13 and the nature of the church.

Mark 13 and the Nature of the Church

We cannot artificially impose a first century apocalyptic worldview onto modern society. What does a responsible interpretation of Mark 13 look like? I will describe the type of church assumed in this chapter.

Here are some guidelines:

- No apocalyptic future-gazing, but confident hope in God's coming future
- No date-setting, but always making the most with the time
- No supernatural rescue from outer space, but faith in the God who will never abandon this world to evil
- No complacent church, but a missionary church committed to service, suffering, and patient endurance
- No escapism or doomsday theology, but responsible ethics in a world of demonic power structures

The church must be an expectant church, yet a patient church; a waiting church, yet a witnessing and active church; a hopeful church, but a suffering church.

Apocalyptic is written for a church that is not content with the way things are. This is also a church that is at odds with the world and is hated by the world. It is a church that has suffered because of its witness to Jesus Christ. It is a church that has been forced to flee for its life, a church that has been tempted to follow "false messiahs" and false prophets but has remained, on the whole, loyal to Christ and the gospel.

Finally, Mark 13 assumes that the church holds a particular view of history, a progressive view. History is progressing toward a conclusion. The aim of history is God himself. The central message of apocalyptic is the final triumph of God over all anti-God powers. Therefore, no earthly utopias based on violence. No idolatrous worship of any political system or nation. No ascribing ultimate value to what is not ultimate. The church and its apocalyptic hope stand as a reminder that only God is God. Sometime in the mysterious future God through Christ will bring in his kingdom, in his own way and on his own terms. How and when this will happen, no one knows. This is the paradox of apocalyptic hope.

Christians must accept the fact that Jesus is coming soon, but not that soon.

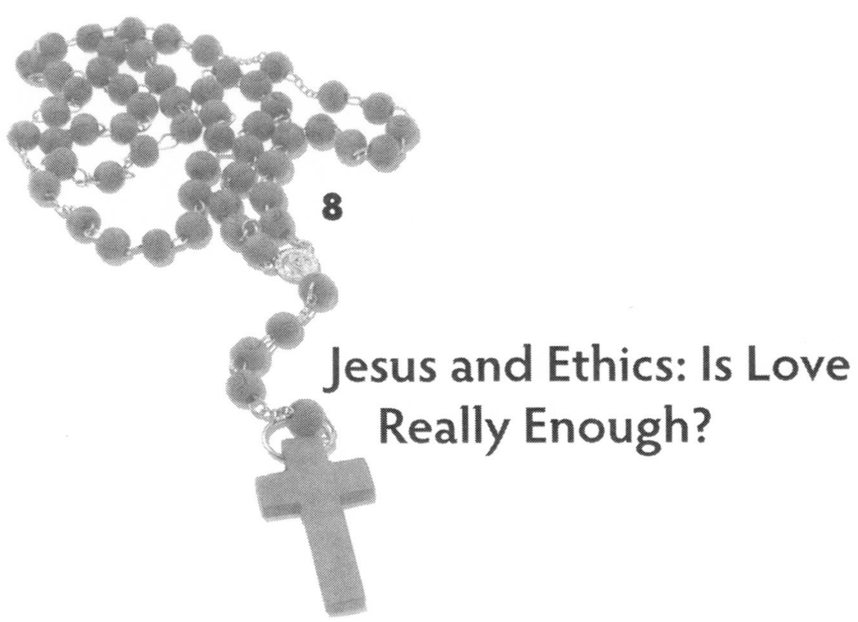

8

Jesus and Ethics: Is Love Really Enough?

Not everyone who says to me, 'Lord, Lord,' will enter the kingdom of heaven, but only the one who does the will of my Father in heaven.

--Matthew 7:21

The ethics of Jesus. Simple? Achievable? Impossible? Unrealistic?

When we think of Jesus we usually think of love. Jesus taught love. Jesus said people should love one another. The "love commandment" is at the heart of his teachings. But is love enough to solve the complex problems of the world? Is love the answer to radical evil? Should people and nations simply love each other and, thus, build a perfect society?

Jesus did more than encourage people to love one another. His ethics were strenuous, his moral teachings rigorous. The ethics of Jesus have been called "the impossible possibility" (Niebuhr 1979). In this essay we will discover two things: (1) Love is a lot harder than we imagine, and, (2) Evil is worse than we think. Jesus was not sentimental. He was realistic about love and evil, and he approached both from an eschatological perspective.

I have organized the ethics of Jesus the following way:

- The Will of God
- The Coming Kingdom
- The Cost of Discipleship
- The Demand of Obedient Love

First, the ethics of Jesus are grounded in his view of the sovereignty of God and his understanding of *God's will.* According to Jesus, every person stands before God and the demand of God. Jesus called on people to repent and do the will of God, not generally but specifically, from person to person and situation to situation. People are called to do the will of God here and now, in this moment, renouncing self-will, obeying God's will. There was no compromise in Jesus on this point.

Second, the ethical teachings of Jesus are related to *the coming kingdom of God,* that is, his eschatological expectation. Eschatology and moral demand are one. God's coming future means the present moment is a time of decision, a crisis of decision. God's future is bearing down on this world and there isn't much time left. The final hour is now! The time for decision is now! This urgency runs through the teachings of Jesus.

Third, Jesus intended to prepare people for entrance into the kingdom of God and a life of discipleship. His rigorous moral demands do not point to asceticism but to full surrender (Bultmann 1958). It is the surrender of all claims, an obedience that exceeds that of the scribes and Pharisees. Discipleship goes beyond commandments and laws. It is a discipleship that is not of this age because it is the life of the coming age, the life of those who are to be "the salt of the earth" and "the light of the world."

Finally, the ethical center for Jesus was love—obedient, disinterested, all-inclusive love. This love views even the enemy as a neighbor. It is a basic attitude of the will. Love does not contend for its own rights, it goes the extra mile without complaining, and freely gives because it has freely received. This love leads to unlimited forgiveness and is nothing less than ultimate concern for the needs of our neighbor.

To sum up,

- Jesus confronted men and women with the will of God in order to prepare them for life in the kingdom of God. The kingdom was dawning now and would soon be realized in its fullness. His disciples would demonstrate this kingdom-life by choosing God over the world, and choosing obedient love over self-will.

Roger H. Crook writes, "Christian morality is decision and action emanating from character that is shaped by a faith relationship with Christ" (Crook 2002:52). I agree. The Christian moral life is the fruit of faith. But Jesus did not lay down rules for every situation. So, when people ask, "What would Jesus do?" we have a nice little problem on our hands! For now, we will focus in more detail on ethics and eschatological expectations.

The Will of God and Eschatological Expectation

Jesus confronted individuals with the will of God as interpreted through the lens of his eschatological expectations. He didn't offer a system of moral philosophy, like virtue ethics or duty ethics or utilitarianism or natural law theory. Nor did Jesus offer a set of new commandments and laws. He was not a new Moses, and the legal mindset was foreign to him. Jesus proclaimed the will of God in light of God's coming future.

Jesus said, "For whoever does the will of my Father in heaven is my brother and sister and mother" (Matt 12:50). He said, "Not everyone who says to me, 'Lord, Lord,' will enter the kingdom of heaven, but only the one who does the will of my Father in heaven" (Matt 7:21). The only life worth living, in his view, was a life committed to doing the will of God. Jesus presented himself as the authoritative voice of the will of God. Every person who heard him preach and teach was confronted with a decision to obey the will of God or not.

Jesus did not teach "original sin." No one is born evil. Rather, Jesus taught that there are good people and bad people, just as there are good trees and bad trees, good soil and bad soil. "The good person brings good things out of a good treasure, and the evil person brings evil things out of an evil treasure" (Matt 12:35). The world is not evil in and of itself; it is human beings who become evil through an evil will. Evil, for Jesus, is rooted in the human will. As Rudolf Bultmann notes, "The real evil in the world, then, is the evil will of men" (Bultmann 1958:50).

Jesus assumed that people are capable of aligning their will with the will of God. The key point is *responsibility*: Jesus assumed people were free moral agents who were responsible for their choices. They could choose obedience or disobedience; they could choose to be sinners or to be righteous. It depended on their will.

This brings us to eschatology. For Jesus, God's future is the controlling factor in the present. This means the present is a turning point. God would soon act to bring in a new world order and to set up his reign. Human beings would never bring in God's kingdom. Only God would do that through a final, apocalyptic Big Bang.

Jesus prayed: "Your kingdom come. Your will be done on earth as it is in heaven" (Matt 6:10). He was praying for God to set up his new world order and vanquish the old order of evil and sin. It is a prayer for the end of the world as we know it. He said, "You know how to interpret the appearance of the sky, but you cannot interpret the signs of the times" (Matt 16:3). The "signs of the times" indicated the end was near.

What does this require of people? If time is running out, what does this require of people? If entering the kingdom is the top priority of life, what does this require of people? Certainly one thing it requires is *renunciation*—the renunciation of self-will. It also implies *freedom*. By faith, the children of the kingdom can live freely, trusting in the loving care of their Father in heaven,

> But strive first for the kingdom of God and his righteousness, and all these things will be given to you as well. So do not worry about tomorrow, for tomorrow will bring worries of its own. Today's trouble is enough for today. (Matt 6:33-34)
>
> Do not be afraid, little flock, for it is your Father's highest delight to give you the kingdom. (Lk 12:32)

Gone is the obsession over securing a future in this transitory world. Gone is the selfish acquisition of wealth as a means of gaining status and security. Gone are the stabbing worries of this life that grow like thorns and choke out the word of God (Mk 4:18-19). Through renunciation and faith in the coming God, the children of the kingdom live freely in this world without succumbing to the ways of the world. They have fastened their hope on the hidden treasure buried in the field and on the pearl of great price (Matt 13:44-46).

Jesus taught many things besides the coming of the Son of Man, but his ethics were about life in the kingdom of God. He laid down the terms for entry into the kingdom and told people how they should live if they wanted to be children of the kingdom. Bart Ehrman writes, "Preparation for the Kingdom—that's what ultimately lies at the heart of Jesus' ethics" (Ehrman 1999:162).

Many of the ethical teachings of Jesus make sense only in light of his apocalyptic expectations. Paul Ramsey points out that Jesus' strenuous teachings such as "non-resisting, unclaiming love, overflowing good even for an enemy, unlimited forgiveness for every offense, giving to every need, unconditional lending to him who would borrow" reveal the effect of his kingdom-expectation (Ramsey 1993:34). Certainly non-resistance to evil would be suicide for a nation, and lending freely to everyone who asks for money would result in bankruptcy. We naturally modify these strenuous demands because, in the long term, they are unrealistic.

All of which means that not even love by itself can overcome the radical power of evil. Ramsey observes,

> Apparently Jesus did not think the way of love, which it was his and his disciples' vocation to practice, would by itself be able to deal with every form of evil, or was all the action needed. It is plain that Jesus considered the area in which evil could be overcome to be a limited one. (Ramsey 1993:37)

Jesus did not expect love to overcome all the evil in the world. He expected *God* to overcome all the evil in the world at the last day. God's righteousness and God's intervention were the ultimate solution to radical evil.

If this is the case, discipleship operates in limited areas where evil can be overcome by good, perhaps incrementally as people respond to the gospel of the kingdom. But ultimately, evil will be vanquished by an apocalyptic firestorm when the Son of Man appears in power and glory. This appears to be what Jesus believed. I want to stress this point, because too often Christians are naïve about love. There is a simplistic attitude of "why can't we all just get along and love each other?" Because evil is quite bad and quite powerful.

Jesus never taught that love would solve the problems of the world. He never taught that universal love will result in world peace. He never taught that love will miraculously result in justice, equality, and freedom for all. Nor did he teach that "all you need is love." Jesus, frankly, was realistic about evil and the distortion of the human will. He had no hope that human beings, through love, could save the world. In his view, only God could save the world, and people had better get ready now, because God was coming soon.

Discipleship and Obedient Love

Now we come to *discipleship.* Is the Christian life a life of keeping commandments and laws? We have already seen that the supreme norm for Jesus was the will of God, not the legalistic keeping of commandments. Jesus presented himself as the interpreter of the will of God. At times he placed himself above Moses and the Jewish law.

Doing the will of God requires more than keeping commandments. Jesus never intended to abolish the Jewish law; he intensified it, as we see in his strident prohibition of divorce, when Moses allowed divorce in certain cases (Mk 10:2-9). At other times, he judged the law as inadequate and spoke on his own authority: "You have heard it said . . . but I say to you." He freely interpreted the Sabbath commandment. He undercut the Jewish laws regarding ritual purity and abolished the distinction between the sacred and the profane,

> Listen to me, all of you, and understand: there is nothing outside a person that by going into him can defile, but the things that come out are what defile. (Mk 7:14-15)

Jesus associated with those "outside the law." These were Jews who did not strictly keep the commandments or follow the letter of the law as taught by the scribes and Pharisees. He ate with tax collectors and sinners and prostitutes. He was severely criticized for this, his enemies saying, "This man welcomes sinners and eats with them" (Lk 15:2).

Regarding the Sabbath, Jesus placed human need above the law. A person might keep the letter of the Sabbath laws and yet ignore human need and works of mercy. The Sabbath controversies in the Gospels revolve around legal requirements versus the demands of love. Love always demands more than commandments.

Holding to the letter of the law is always less than love requires. Love overspills the law and goes further than the law. Human need takes priority over commandments and laws: "The Sabbath was made for humankind, and not humankind for the Sabbath" (Mk 2:27). Or as Hans Kung writes, "Love is good in all situations" (Kung 1978:560).

A person might keep the commandments and still not do the will of God. It is easy to hide behind legalistic obedience to commandments while shirking the duties of love! A rich young man came to Jesus, asking about eternal life. This man was a devout Jew who kept the commandments, but Jesus confronted him with the will of God: "If you would be perfect, go sell your possessions and give the money to the poor, and you will have treasure in heaven; then come, follow me" (Matt 19:21). The man refused the call to discipleship. He rejected the will of God and returned to keeping the commandments.

Gunther Bornkamm remarks, "He [Jesus] liberates the will of God from its petrification in tables of stone, and reaches for the heart of man which seeks seclusion and safety behind the stronghold of observance of the law" (Bornkamm 1960:105). Jesus did not lay down a body of commandments for people to obey. He acted by his own authority and placed himself above the Jewish law. The will of God cannot be entirely embodied in law. The will of God cuts to the core of the human heart and demands the submission of the whole person to the law of love.

In the Sermon on the Mount we are confronted with the pure, undiluted will of God (Matt 5-7). Jesus expected action. He laid down the requirements for discipleship. Jesus was speaking to individuals about their duties as children of the kingdom. He said to his disciples, "You are the salt of the earth . . . You are the light of the world . . . let your light shine before others that they may see your works and give glory to your Father in heaven" (Matt 5:13-16). His followers are called to live a certain way, a radical way.

Jesus spoke about reconciliation between neighbors, adultery, divorce, and oath-taking (Matt 5:21-37). Again, these teachings are aimed at *individuals* and describe how children of the kingdom are to conduct their personal affairs.

A key phrase in the Sermon on the Mount is "so that you may be children of your Father in heaven" (Matt 5:45). God sends sunshine on the evil as well as the good, and God sends rain on the righteous as well as on the unrighteous. Love, in other words, should be unconditional and disinterested: Love those who are not like you, love inclusively, love without expecting a reward, love those who hate you and insult you, welcome everyone, not just your friends. This is all-inclusive, kingdom-love for the neighbor, and "neighbor" includes enemies. Why should we love this way? Because God does: "Be perfect, therefore, as your heavenly Father is perfect" (Matt 5:48).

Jesus was creating a new type of human being. He was setting up a new standard of morality grounded in God and God's new world order. This counter-culture would be the new "people of God." They would live in the world but be governed by other values than those of the world. Not world flight, not monkish asceticism, not violent revolution, but a radical mode of existence: disinterested love for one's neighbor.

Standing for Something

To what extent are the strenuous ethics of Jesus still valid today? This question confronts us with what Paul Ramsey calls "the functional limitation of their validity" (Ramsey 1993:35).

Is the love commandment enough? Reinhold Niebuhr said that Jesus sets before us "the impossible possibility." The paradox of the Christian moral life is that we strive to meet a standard we will never achieve in this life. Here are a few suggestions aimed at resolving this paradox.

First, Jesus never said that love would bring in the kingdom of God. He never said that the coming of the kingdom was dependent on how well people loved one another. God alone would take care of evil at the last day. The future is not under human control; the future is under the sovereignty of God. Jesus believed God would wrap things up, regardless of whether or not people repented and loved one another. Jesus called individuals to discipleship, not nations and kingdoms.

Second, the apocalyptic dream of Jesus did not come to pass. Moreover, most modern persons do not share the apocalyptic horizon of Jesus; we no longer expect the Son of Man to appear from outer space. How do we affirm the ethical teachings of Jesus when those teachings were grounded in his apocalyptic expectations? The church has been doing just this for centuries. Christian ethics evolved to suit a new, non-apocalyptic situation. This means discernment from context to context, from situation to situation, and from culture to culture. Christians must apply more broadly the basic principles underlying the ethics of Jesus.

Reinhold Niebuhr writes that we are left with the problem "of creating and maintaining tentative harmonies of life in the world in terms of the possibilities of the human situation, while yet at the same time preserving the indictment upon all human life of the impossible possibility, the law of love" (1979:37). In a fallen world, "tentative harmonies" are the most we can expect. Yet such harmonies must be rooted in Jesus' ethic of love and his commitment to God's will and to humanity.

Finally, the ethics of Jesus require people to take a stand and to live cruciform lives. We must not forget that Jesus died on the cross for God's cause and for humanity's cause. He took a stand against evil and evil political powers. He was killed by the combined powers of church and state. If he had not been such a religious and political threat, he would not have been crucified.

Standing for something—this is what discipleship means. Cruciform living is life shaped by the cross. Discipleship means action in a world that is not committed to the will of God or to God's kingdom. Nations, corporations, and other power structures are not committed to God's kingdom. Therefore, confrontation with "the powers" is inevitable.

Jesus did not address every moral problem, but he set down kingdom values, and he confronted people with the will of God. We can only approximate what Jesus would do. From situation to situation, from person to person, we can only approximate the ethics of Jesus. But a few things are clear. Ethics is about responding to the will of God as it confronts us in the concrete need of our neighbor. Christian ethics is a response to neighbor-need in light of God's demand. It is clear that Christians are commanded to come down on the side of humanity. God is on the side of humanity. Christians must be on the side of humanity also.

Even after doing our best—sometimes choosing the lesser of two evils—"every actuality of history reveals itself, after the event, as only an approximation of the ideal; and the Kingdom of God is therefore not here. It is, in fact, always coming but never here" (Niebuhr 1979:36).

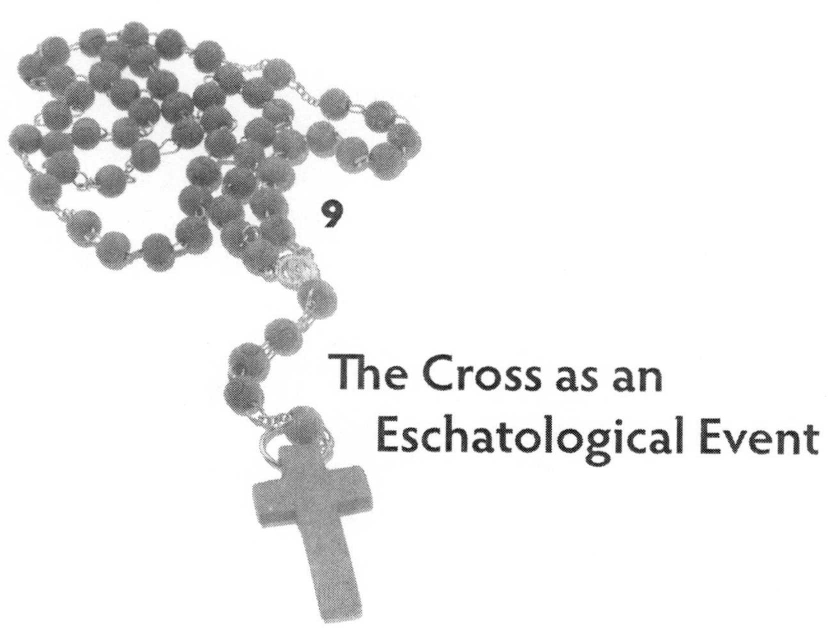

9

The Cross as an Eschatological Event

"In the cross of Christ I glory, towering o'er the wrecks of time . . ." The words of this old hymn still ring true for Christians and give birth to Christian hope. The cross is the central symbol of Christian faith. It is there that God's love and grace are revealed as never before, and the historical present meets God's new future. The New Testament views the cross as an eschatological turning point.

Christianity began as a failure. It began with the death of Jesus on the cross and the anguish of disappointed dreams. The disciples believed that Jesus was the Messiah who would bring in the New Age and restore glory to Israel. The cross was an embarrassment. It appeared that Jesus was cursed by God, a messianic pretender and false prophet. A crucified Messiah was a bizarre way for God to save the world.

We are about to explore the death of Jesus in the Gospel of Mark. How is the cross related to the kingdom of God, eternal life, and the New Creation? To what extent did Jesus view his death as necessary for the coming of the kingdom? In what way is the cross a saving event?

About one-third of Mark is devoted to the suffering and death of Jesus. Jesus is the suffering servant of God who gives up his life for the kingdom of God and offers a vicarious sacrifice for the salvation of the world, "to give his life as a ransom for many" (Mk 10:45). Jesus said, "This is my blood of the covenant, which is poured out for many" (Mk 14:24). The death of Jesus is related to God's end-time salvation.

We must go back to those days and revisit the story as told by Mark.

Collision and Impending Doom

The time is fulfilled, and the kingdom of God has come near; repent, and believe the good news.

--Mark 1:15

Mark views Jesus as the latter-day prophet of the kingdom announcing "the last days" and the need to repent, believe, and enter the kingdom of God before it's too late. From the beginning, Jesus announces an eschatological message: "The time is fulfilled, and the kingdom of God has come near; repent, and believe the good news" (Mk 1:15). The long wait is over! Promise has led to fulfillment! But not everyone was excited to hear this news.

Jesus is portrayed as a trouble maker. He collides with the religious establishment. The death of Jesus becomes the death of a "prophet-martyr" who was sent to Israel but was rejected like many prophets before him. To Mark, Jesus is the eschatological prophet of the last days, condemned by religious leaders who believe they are doing God's will.

This interpretation of the death of Jesus is the earliest and the one most aligned with "the concrete facts" (Schillebeeckx 1979:281). It is grounded in the long Jewish prophetic tradition that can be summarized as "Israel kills its prophets." The Old Testament paints a picture of Israel resisting its prophets and rejecting God's call to repentance. According to Mark, Jesus is Israel's final prophet announcing the final hour before the end.

The death of Jesus is grounded in his conflict with the Jewish establishment (Kung 1992:333). We see Jesus arguing with the Pharisees, Sadducees, scribes, Herodians, and the chief priests. He is an outsider who doesn't get along with anyone in a position of authority. Like an Old Testament prophet, Jesus confronts power, critiques power, and collides with power. He speaks the message of God with an authority that astounds his listeners (Mk 1:22, 27). His authority threatens the religious establishment that is based on the Torah, the temple, and the traditions of the elders. Yet Jesus assumes that God is speaking through him and working through him. He interprets the Jewish scriptures freely, according to his own opinions. His opponents challenge him by asking, "By what authority are you doing these things? Who gave you this authority to do them?" (Mk 11:28).

Thus, the central conflict of Mark's Gospel is the issue of authority: *the authority of Jesus versus the authority of the Jewish establishment.* This is why Jesus is killed. Here is a new prophet announcing a new time with new authority. He interprets Jewish law with remarkable freedom and clashes with "the guardians of the law" by placing himself above Moses and the Torah (Moltmann 1974:129). He is accused of being a false teacher and leading the people astray.

Jesus also performs powerful deeds and associates with those "outside the law," the cast-offs and "sinners." He says, "No one puts new wine into old wineskins; otherwise, the wine will burst the skins, and the wine is lost, and so are the skins; but one puts new wine into fresh wineskins (Mk 2:22). The message of Jesus is "new wine" that requires a new attitude, a new perspective, and a fresh openness to the kingdom of God as it is being revealed in Jesus and his miraculous works. Jesus proclaims a new kind of righteousness. This righteousness is defined by the freedom of God to show grace to whomever he chooses, regardless of the law and its requirements (Moltmann 1993:132).

Jesus criticized "the traditions of the elders" (Mk 7:1-13). He downplayed Jewish purity laws, fasting, Sabbath observance, table fellowship, and the temple. Shockingly, Jesus distinguished between the will of God and the Jewish law. Meticulous observance of the law does not necessarily equate with the will of God. Jesus attacked Pharisaic righteousness and confronted it with the will of God: "Whoever does the will of God is my brother and sister and mother" (3:35). He said, "Watch out—beware of the yeast of the Pharisees and the yeast of Herod" (8:15). Yeast is a symbol of corrupt teaching.

This trouble-maker raised a lot of questions in people's minds. Was Jesus an eschatological prophet or an imposter?

Not even the disciples were free of ambivalence. Some people thought that Jesus was John the Baptist brought back from the dead, or maybe Elijah the prophet, or one of the prophets from long ago (Mk 6:14-16; 8:27-28). This "historical ambivalence" about Jesus is not cleared up until after the resurrection (Schillebeeckx 1979: 280). It doesn't help, however, that Jesus concealed his identity as the Messiah. This has been called "the Messianic secret." Jesus is unwilling to admit that he is the Messiah, and he will not permit others to do it (Mk 1:34; cf. 1:44; 3:11-12; 5:43; 7:36; 8:30; 9:9, 30). *Jesus never refers to himself as the Messiah.* Hans Kung writes,

> Only in the light of the Easter experience could one clearly see the Jesus tradition in a messianic light and thus introduce the messianic confession into the account of the history of Jesus. And before that? Jesus' proclamation and praxis had hardly matched the messianic expectations of his contemporaries which were contradictory and mostly theo-political—most of the rabbis, too, expected a triumphant messiah. (Kung 1992:331)

Jesus was accused of blasphemy (Mk 14:34). The scribes exclaim, "Why does this fellow speak in this way? It is blasphemy!" (Mk 2:7). Blasphemy implies self-deification or claiming for oneself powers that belong to God alone. The charge of blasphemy is central to Jesus' condemnation and ultimate death. From a religious point of view, Jesus was condemned to death for being a blasphemer, a false prophet, a lying teacher, and a deceiver of the people.

Impending Doom

Mark is driven by suspense toward the cross. Everything leads up to Jesus' death, step by step, argument by argument. Tension builds. We know Jesus is going to die. There is no way he can continue doing what he's doing without getting killed.

The shadow of impending doom hovers over Mark's narrative. Mark begins with the preaching of John the Baptist (Mk 1:1-8). John was a radical reformer, a fiery preacher, another outsider proclaiming repentance and baptism as preparatory steps to the coming of the Messiah (see Chapter Five). John was beheaded by Herod (Mk 6:14-29). This did not go unnoticed by Jesus, who must have realized that he, too, would likely be murdered.

Following his baptism, Jesus began his mission in Galilee, removed from the center of power. Jesus announced repentance and the nearness of the kingdom of God (Mk 1:15). He called disciples to follow him (Mk 1:16-20). He taught with authority in the synagogues of Galilee, healed the sick, cast out demons, revealed amazing divine powers, and challenged the traditions of the elders (Mk 1:21-34; 2:18-22). In one story, Jesus healed a paralytic and forgave his sins, which was interpreted as blasphemy (Mk 2:1-12).

Jesus associated with tax collectors and sinners, eating with people who were "unclean" and who ignored Jewish purity laws (Mk 2:15-17). Such table fellowship with "sinners" was a foretaste of the Messianic banquet at the end of time. It revealed "the boundary-breaking mission of compassion" we see in Jesus (Senior 1984:23).

Jesus and his disciples did not fast like the Pharisees (Mk 2:18-20). Jesus challenged the traditional customs regarding the Sabbath. His disciples picked grain on the Sabbath and, when criticized, Jesus set himself up as "lord" of the Sabbath (Mk 2:28). He healed a man with a withered hand on the Sabbath (Mk 3:1-5). Immediately after these events, the Pharisees and Herodians conspired to kill Jesus (Mk 3:6). Later, the chief priests and scribes plot to kill him (Mk 11:18; 14:1).

Jesus was accused of demon possession (Mk 3:19-30). He was rejected in Nazareth, his home town (Mk 6:1-6). He warned his disciples that their message will not be welcome in certain towns and villages (Mk 6:11). He collided with the religious authorities regarding Jewish food laws and condemned them for setting aside "the commandments of God" in order to follow their own manmade traditions (Mk 7:1-13). He went out of his way to preach the "good news" to Gentiles living in Tyre and Sidon (Mk 7:24-30). These events took place in Galilee. Jesus had not yet gone to Jerusalem.

A turning point occurred in Caesarea Philippi (Mk 8:27-30). This story marks a transition in the Gospel of Mark. This is the moment when Peter declares that Jesus is the Messiah. Immediately Jesus began to teach the disciples that the Messiah must suffer and die, and after three days, rise again (Mk 8:31). Peter would have none of this! A crucified Messiah is not part of his idea of success. Jesus rebuked Peter harshly. He made it clear that the death of the Messiah was part of God's plan (Mk 8:32-34).

Jesus was following a divine imperative. He came to believe that he must suffer and die in order to bring in God's eschatological kingdom. Mark uses the title "Son of Man," a title borrowed from Daniel and carrying eschatological overtones. The Son of Man must be betrayed into the hands of sinners, suffer and die, and be raised on the third day (Mk 8:31; 9:9, 12; 10:33-34, 45; 14:21, 41). Jesus certainly did not view himself as a political Messiah. What is new in his teaching is that the long-hoped for Messiah is none other than the Son of Man who will bring in the kingdom at the end of the age. This Son of Man is none other than himself. He must die according to God's plan. These are *apocalyptic* ideas: Jesus must suffer prior to "the end" to open the way for the final arrival of God's kingdom in power. This would be an eschatological death marking the end of the age and the beginning of the New Age.

He *must* go to Jerusalem.

Jerusalem Showdown

> *They were on the road, going up to Jerusalem, and Jesus was walking ahead of them; they were amazed, and those who followed were afraid.*
>
> --*Mark 10:32*

Mark gives us the basic outline of the final week of Jesus' life:

- Triumphal entry
- Cleansing of the temple
- Teaching in the temple
- Last Supper/Gethsemane
- Arrest/Trial/Crucifixion

Gunther Bornkamm notes that Jesus went to Jerusalem to confront the people there with his message of the coming kingdom, "and to summon them at the eleventh hour to make their decision" (Bornkamm 1960:155). Jesus went to Jerusalem for a confrontation, not to make a gentle appeal. He was not naïve; he knew he had "a baptism to be baptized with," and this meant suffering and death (Mk 10:38).

The triumphal entry into Jerusalem was an intentional messianic procession (Mk 11:1-12). It excited the passions of the people and fueled their dream for a Davidic king. Such a public display of religious zeal would provoke a response either by the Romans or the Jewish leaders. It was Passover. Jerusalem was filled with pilgrims, and the Roman soldiers were on high alert.

The triumphal entry had serious political overtones. This was highhanded treason. Jesus was setting off a keg of political dynamite: "Without this popular excitement, his crucifixion by the Romans as 'king of the Jews' would be incomprehensible" (Moltmann 1990:160).

The following day Jesus entered the temple and turned over the tables of the money-changers (Mk 11:15-19). He took over the outer court of the temple, asserted his authority and suspended the purchasing of sacrificial animals. This was the act that sealed his fate. Judaism could tolerate messianic pretenders, but Jesus struck at the heart of Jewish faith and life: *the temple, the priesthood, and the sacrificial system*. It is possible that Jesus went to Jerusalem to confront the temple cult, the center of religious power. He went to confront a religion run by priests and aristocrats. For Jesus, the temple and its sacrifices had become superfluous and irrelevant in light of the approaching kingdom of God. He did not talk about reforming the temple; rather, the temple would be destroyed (another apocalyptic idea). The reign of God meant the end of the Jewish temple and priesthood.

Prior to his arrest, Jesus predicted the destruction of the temple (Mk 13:1-2). At his trial, he was accused of speaking against the temple (Mk 14:58). As he hung on the cross, he was mocked regarding his statements about the temple (Mk 15:29). When Jesus died, the curtain of the temple was torn in half, a symbol of the end of the temple cult and the sacrificial system (Mk 15:38). To strike at the Torah and the temple was to threaten the heart of Jewish faith and life. Jesus did both.

For a few days Jesus taught in the temple. He told a parable about "the wicked tenants" (Mk 12:1-12). The story revolves around a landowner who sends his servants to certain tenants. The wicked tenants keep killing the messengers until they finally kill the landowner's son. Jesus used this parable to illustrate the long history of rejection between God's prophets and God's people, Israel. The message is clear: "Israel kills its prophets!" Jesus is about to become one more rejected prophet. Following this parable, the Jewish leaders wanted to arrest Jesus, but they feared the crowd (Mk 12:12).

On his final night, Jesus met with his disciples for a final meal. At that meal, Jesus took a glass of wine and said,

> This is my blood of the covenant, which is poured out for many. Truly I tell you, I will never again drink of the fruit of the vine until that day when I drink it new in the kingdom of God. (Mk 14:24-25)

Obviously, Jesus viewed his death as central to the imminent arrival of the kingdom of God in power. Through his death the kingdom would finally arrive, the Son of Man would appear, and there would be a resurrection and judgment to follow. Jesus did not envision a long period of time before the end. Therefore, even if he died, he and his message would be confirmed by God in the end-time events soon to follow (Pannenberg 1968:54-55). He was asking his disciples to trust him. After his suffering, he would see them again in the kingdom—soon.

In the Garden of Gethsemane, Jesus wrestled with his fears (Mk 14:32-42). Mark tells us that Jesus "began to be distressed and agitated." The words literally mean "to quake and shiver." Jesus began to fall apart as he realized what he was facing. Gethsemane is "the frightening eclipse of God" (Moltmann 1990:166). But Jesus surrendered to God's will. He chose to drink the cup of God-forsakenness on the cross.

Jesus was arrested by the temple police and taken before the high priest and Sanhedrin (Mk 14:43-65). Here, for the first time, he openly admitted to being the Messiah. Combined with his attitude toward the law and the temple, this was enough to condemn him as a blasphemer. Jurgen Moltmann comments:

> It emerged from the nocturnal cross-examination that Jesus really did consider himself to be the messiah, and was not prepared to renounce his claim in spite of everything that spoke against it. He was then presumably condemned as a blasphemous messianic pretender. Yet at the same time he was judged to be so dangerous politically that he was handed over to the Romans, on the grounds that he wanted to set himself up as 'king of the Jews.' (Moltmann 1990:162)

According to Mark, Jesus was sent from the high priest to Pilate and was accused of "many things" (Mk 15:3). Why should Pilate care? These Jews meant nothing to him, and Jesus meant nothing to him. But Pilate was a pragmatist and a despot. The last thing he wanted was an insurrection caused by a Jewish Galilean fanatic. Here we find the phrase "king of the Jews" used five times and "king of Israel" used once (Mk 15:2, 9, 11, 18, 26, 32). This was a political charge. Jesus never claimed to be king of the Jews, but this was the official charge brought against him. That charge was nailed onto the cross with him. The political charge was *treason*: usurping the authority of Caesar by claiming to be "king of the Jews."

There is little doubt that Jesus was delivered over to Pilate by the Sanhedrin out of fear of Roman retaliation should things get out of hand. If Jesus created any more problems among the people, there might be a riot and the Romans would crack down. To save the nation, Jesus must die. He was too volatile to keep around. The religious reasons for Jesus' death, as we have seen, include his attack on the law and the temple, and blasphemy.

In Mark's Gospel, Jesus dies the death of a Godforsaken prophet-martyr.

More Than A Prophet-Martyr

He has been raised; he is not here.

--Mark 16:6

Mark offers no systematic interpretation of the cross. He simply states that the death of Jesus is a "ransom for many." Ransom from what? The implication is that Jesus died for others. *Vicarious suffering* becomes the central theme of the cross.

What we can say is this:

- The cross was not an accident
- The cross was the inevitable outcome of Jesus' messianic mission
- The cross was an eschatological event related to the kingdom of God
- The cross has permanent validity and saving significance for Christians

Jesus died as a "prophet-martyr" who gave his life for what he believed to be God's cause, in the hope of future vindication.

But wasn't Jesus more than a prophet-martyr? Isn't he essentially different from all other prophets who preceded him? Wasn't his death the death of *God's Son*? Yet this was not clear until afterwards, that is, until the resurrection.

Throughout Jesus' public life, future confirmation was always needed and called for. Not even his deeds of power were enough to prove his claims; they confirmed the beginning of the kingdom of God, but not fully or completely (Pannenberg 1968:53). In other words, Jesus' claims anticipated future verification by God. The cross was a disconfirmation! The cross implied that Jesus was a fraud. Consequently, the cross by itself is a tragedy that offers no hope.

This brings us to the resurrection. Mark doesn't spend much

time on the resurrection. There is no doubt, however, that the resurrection is the confirming event of Jesus' pre-Easter life (see Chapter Ten). "He has been raised; he is not here"—these words mark the next stage of salvation history. The resurrection is God's endorsement of everything Jesus said and did. The resurrection means that Jesus was right and "the guardians of the law" were wrong. Jesus was who he claimed to be: the authoritative voice of God for the latter days, the Son of God, the Messiah

The death of Jesus has permanent validity and saving significance only when viewed in light of the resurrection. The Christian interpretation of the cross begins with the resurrection. Apart from the resurrection, Jesus remains only a prophet-martyr, another inspirational dead hero.

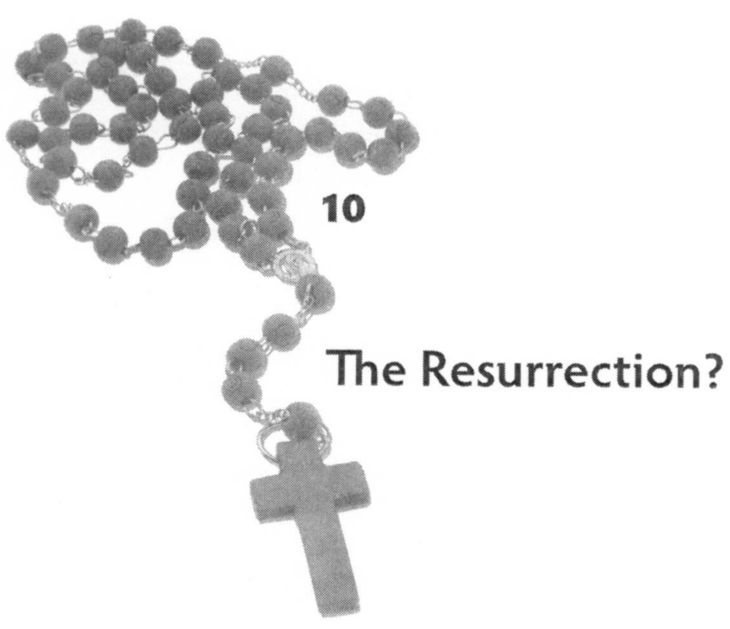

10

The Resurrection?

But God raised him up, having freed him from death, because it was impossible for him to be held in its power.
--Acts 2:24

Christian faith began with an experience: the resurrection of Jesus from the dead.

Shortly after his crucifixion, certain followers of Jesus experienced him as alive. This is the beginning of Christian faith. Everything else came later—theology, dogmas, creeds, church structures—but the resurrection was the event that gave birth to Christianity.

Christian faith is resurrection faith. The stunning acclamation of Christian faith is "Jesus is alive, and Jesus is Lord!" This proclamation is based on the testimony of those "witnesses" of the resurrection. One of those persons was Paul, who offers the oldest summary of Christian faith,

> For I handed on to you as of first importance what I in turn had received: that Christ died for our sins in accordance

> with the scriptures, and that he was buried, and that he was raised on the third day in accordance with the scriptures, and that he appeared to Cephas [Peter], then to the twelve. (1 Cor 15:3-5)

Dead, buried, raised, appeared—this is the creedal formula, the heart of the Christian gospel. By the fifth century (in Spain and Gaul), the Apostles' Creed emerged as a succinct statement of Christian faith. Christ, it says, "suffered under Pontius Pilate, was crucified, died, and was buried; he descended to the dead; on the third day he rose again; he ascended into heaven and is seated at the right hand of the Father."

Easter faith is post-resurrection faith. Again, the Apostle Paul:

> If Christ has not been raised, then our proclamation has been in vain and your faith has been in vain. (1 Cor 15:14)
>
> We know that Christ, being raised from the dead, will never die again; death no longer has dominion over him. (Rom 6:9)
>
> I want to know Christ and the power of his resurrection and the sharing of his sufferings by becoming like him in his death, if somehow I may attain the resurrection from the dead. (Phil 3:10-11)

In the New Testament, the resurrection is something God does, and it is specifically related to Jesus. The resurrection is about God and about Jesus. More specifically, it is a statement by God *about* Jesus.

Furthermore, the resurrection is an eschatological event, the foretaste of the resurrection of the dead at the end of time. Because Christ has been raised, a new time now exists. The resurrection means that God's new future has already begun.

There are difficulties and misunderstandings, however. The resurrection of Christ is ambiguous, and there is room for doubt. We will explore the difficulties with the resurrection of Christ, most of them based on misconceptions. We need to be clear about what the resurrection is and what it is not. We will also focus on the positive content of the Easter message.

What It Isn't

It is the Lord!

--John 21:7

First, we must clarify what the resurrection of Christ is *not*. It is not:

- The immortality of the soul
- A historical event like other events
- The resuscitation of a corpse
- Mystical rebirth

Let's work through these one at a time.

The immortality of the soul? This is a Greek idea, not Hebrew, and it is not the biblical understanding of human nature. Jewish and Christian anthropology views the human being as a unit, an indivisible union of body and spirit. God created us as embodied spirits. The body is not evil but is an essential component of who we are. Some might believe that the immortal soul of Jesus left his body and flew off to be with God, but that isn't the New Testament view. Jesus was raised from the dead and was seen by his followers as a real person with a body that could be touched and seen. Granted, his body was different, but there was still a body of some sort. The resurrection of Christ has nothing to do with belief in the immortality of the soul. It has everything to do with the crucified Jesus being raised up as a total person and exalted into the presence of God, not as an immortal soul but as a living, spiritual body.

A historical event? There were no reporters at the tomb to record the resurrection. There were no eyewitnesses. No one can describe what happened. Unlike the crucifixion, a public event in history, the resurrection was not a public event. Historians cannot verify the resurrection as an event within history, like other events. We know only that the tomb was empty and numerous followers of Jesus experienced him as alive. The empty tomb is not proof. At best, the empty tomb is dubious supplemental evidence of the resurrection. The Easter message is about the living Christ, not the empty tomb. The empty tomb can mean many things, but it does not prove the resurrection.

The resurrection is not accessible to the methods of historical research. Therefore, it is not a historical event in the normal sense.

The resuscitation of a corpse? The New Testament is clear on this point: *the living Christ is not a resuscitated corpse.* There is nothing in the resurrection stories to imply that Jesus came out of the tomb with the same biological body he had when he went in. Nor was he resurrected in order to die again like everyone else. Death was once and for all behind him. His resurrection was entirely different from other resurrections, which are really "reanimations," not resurrections. Jesus was not reanimated. He was resurrected, "the first to rise from the dead," according to Paul (Acts 26:23). It was a first. This sets the resurrection apart from the raising of Jairus's daughter and the raising of Lazarus (see Mk 5:35-43; Jn 11:17-44). Jesus did not come forth from the tomb as "flesh and blood," yet he appeared as a "spiritual body," an "imperishable" body (1 Cor 15:42-49).

Mystical rebirth? The New Testament does not spiritualize the resurrection of Christ or turn it into mystical rebirth. The disciples were not talking about mystical rebirth, as if to say "Jesus has been resurrected in my heart." They encountered Jesus as a living person: "It is the Lord!" The resurrection stories emphasize the continuity between Jesus and the risen Christ. The crucified Jesus from Galilee is the risen Christ. They are one and the same person. This does not rule out mysticism as part of Christian spirituality, but it keeps Christianity from becoming a mystical religion based on the subjective experiences of the individual. Essentially, Christian spirituality is grounded in the death and resurrection of Jesus Christ two thousand years ago.

Thus, the resurrection of Christ is not the immortality of the soul, or a historical event like other events, or the resuscitation of a corpse, or mystical rebirth. Then what is it?

What It Is

> *Therefore let the entire house of Israel know with certainty that God has made him both Lord and Messiah, this Jesus who you crucified.*
>
> *--Acts 2:36*

How did a new religion emerge after the disaster of the crucifixion? Jesus was executed as a heretic, a seducer of the people, a false Messiah, an insurrectionist, and a God-forsaken failure. His followers were crushed. All indicators pointed to a grand fiasco. The cross appeared to be God's judgment on Jesus as an imposter. Here was a man who claimed much for himself but who died a shameful death, without God! How, then, was Christianity born?

The answer? *Easter.*

Christian faith is post-resurrection faith: *faith in the resurrected Jesus who is the Messiah.* The New Testament is written from the perspective of post-resurrection faith. The Gospels are post-resurrection documents. Christian reflection on the significance of Jesus began after the resurrection, and Christian theology begins with Easter and works backwards. Christology begins with Easter and asks,

- Who is this person whom God raised from the dead? Why is he significant for history and human destiny?

The meaning of the resurrection of Christ can be divided into four parts:

- Vindication
- Exaltation
- Vocation
- Hope

Vindication. The resurrection of the righteous at the end of time is an apocalyptic idea related to vindication. Why do the righteous suffer, and is there a reward beyond the grave, beyond the injustices of this world? What about martyrs who die for their faith? What about God's people who are persecuted while the wicked prosper? The fact is, all accounts are not settled at death. Will there come a time when all accounts are settled? Will God's faithful people be vindicated at last? Can God be trusted to do what's just? These are questions of *theodicy*—the relation between an unjust world and a just God.

Through the resurrection, God sets the record straight once and for all. This Jewish apocalyptic idea was inherited by Christianity via Jesus. We first encounter an unambiguous reference to the resurrection in the book of Daniel,

> Many of those who sleep in the dust of the earth shall awake, some to everlasting life, and some to shame and everlasting contempt. Those who are wise shall shine like the brightness of the sky, and those who lead many to righteousness, like the stars forever and ever. (Dan 12:2-3)

These words were written in the 2nd century B.C. under intense persecution of Jews by Antiochus IV Epiphanes (see Chapter Three). Resurrection was about ultimate justice and vindication. If those who stayed true to the Torah and died for their faith had no hope beyond the grave, where is justice and vindication? If the persecutors of God's people were never arraigned before a final judgment, where is justice and vindication? Resurrection was the answer. God would vindicate his people through the resurrection at the end of time.

Two of the most important promises of the messianic age were the resurrection of the dead and the vindication of God's righteous people (Fredricksen 2000:133-134). In the resurrection of Jesus, his followers saw both promises fulfilled. To them, the resurrection was the official beginning of the New Age, the official beginning of a restored Israel with the risen Christ taking the lead. The last days had arrived. Christians already share in "the glory to be revealed" (1 Pt 5:1). They have already tasted "the powers of the age to come" (Heb 6:5). Paul viewed the resurrection of Christ as "the first fruits" of the universal resurrection (1 Cor 15:20).

Not only this, the resurrection of Jesus the Crucified means that the life and message of Jesus of Nazareth are *permanently valid.* His death is "a death into the resurrection" because his life and message are permanently valid for all time and beyond time (Rahner 1978: 266). Therefore, the resurrection of Christ was God's vindication of Jesus and everything he stood for. It was God saying, "Jesus was right all along." Jesus is "the faithful witness" to God's character, God's passion, God's will, and God's kingdom (Rev 1:5). This is the central point of Peter's sermon at Pentecost (Acts 2:14-36). To paraphrase, Peter said, "You counted Jesus worthy of death and killed him as a heretic, but God raised him up and declared him to be Lord and Messiah. You're wrong, Jesus was right, and Jesus now reigns for all time and beyond time!" The resurrection is God's seal of approval on Jesus now and forever, and the vindication of Jesus the Crucified is also the vindication of those who entrust themselves to Christ in faith.

This brings us to the idea of exaltation.

Exaltation. After the resurrection, did Jesus literally sit down "at the right hand of God"? What does exaltation mean? The New Testament views resurrection and exaltation as one event, though they are distinct. Jesus was raised from the dead and exalted into the life of God. This is symbolic language describing a dimension beyond space and time. To say that Jesus "ascended to God" or is "seated at God's right hand" point to *cosmic authority.* We are told that Jesus "has gone into heaven and is at the right hand of God, with angels, authorities, and powers made subject to him" (1 Pt 3:22). That is, Jesus is Lord. He has been granted cosmic authority as Messiah, Savior, Lord, and Judge. He is "the ruler of the kings of the earth" (Rev 1:5).

At Pentecost Peter proclaimed, "Therefore let the entire house of Israel know with certainty that God has made him both Lord and Messiah" (Acts 2:36). Paul writes that Jesus was "declared to be Son of God with power according to the spirit of holiness by resurrection from the dead, Jesus Christ our Lord" (Rom 1:4). An ancient Christian hymn proclaims:

> Therefore God also highly exalted him and gave him the name that is above every name, so that at the name of Jesus every knee should bend, in heaven and on earth and under the earth, and every tongue should confess that Jesus Christ is Lord, to the glory of God the Father. (Phil 2:9-11)

Exaltation is an eschatological symbol of the cosmic authority of Jesus Christ, crucified, resurrected, and reigning as Lord. Marcus Borg stresses this point when he writes, "To affirm that Jesus is Lord is to deny all other lords" (Borg 2003:54). The Lordship of Christ challenges all earthly authorities and domination systems. Yet Jesus is Lord not only in things pertaining to this life but also the life to come, that is, *human destiny*. The glorified Christ revealed himself to John the Revelator, saying, "Do not be afraid; I am the first and the last, and the living one. I was dead, and see, I am alive forever and ever; and I have the keys of Death and of Hades" (Rev 1:17-18). "Hades" is a metaphor for the realm of the dead. The implication is that Christ is Lord of both the living and the dead, and human destiny is tied to him (see Chapter Eighteen).

Two implications arise from this confession: vocation and hope.

Vocation and Hope

As the Father has sent me, so I send you.

--John 20:21

The resurrection of Christ was the beginning of Christian mission. The main vocation of Christians is to follow Jesus and to bear witness to him throughout the world, to proclaim the "good news" of God's salvation in Christ. The followers of Jesus were not to stand around looking into the empty tomb or into the sky, waiting for Jesus to return in glory. The disciples were called to be witnesses to the world:

- As the Father has sent me, so I send you. (Jn 20:21)
- You will receive power when the Holy Spirit has come upon you; and you will be my witnesses in Jerusalem, in all Judea and Samaria, and to the ends of the earth. (Acts 1:8)
- Go therefore and make disciples of all nations . . . And remember, I am with you always, to the end of the age. (Matt 28:19-20)

The church's primary purpose is mission: to proclaim the gospel of the resurrected Messiah. But here we must be clear. Christians don't view Jesus as a inspirational hero from the past who left a few good teachings behind him. Jesus is more than a role model. He is the resurrected Lord, alive and active through the Spirit in the church and in the world. We might say that Christians follow the risen Christ, not the historical Jesus. Christianity is not "Jesusology." Paul was not primarily interested in the historical Jesus or any kind of biography of Jesus. The Christ Paul followed was the risen Jesus who was crucified and who now reigns as Lord.

Therefore, the Easter message is about *vocation*. This means sharing the fate of Jesus, sharing in his sufferings (Phil 3:10; 1 Pt 4:13).

Paul refers to this as "the obedience of faith" (Rom 1:5; 16:26). How shall we respond to the crucified Jesus who is the risen Lord and who is alive? Is there not an obligation to follow him? *A mission*?

The message of Christian mission is about life. Again and again as a hospice chaplain, I am on the front lines of death and dying. I see people die without hope, and I see people die with hope. I see people die without faith and die in faith. If I cannot offer hope to suffering and dying people, I have no business doing what I'm doing. This hope is grounded in the resurrection of Jesus Christ from the dead. It is a hope that is stronger than death and that goes beyond the grave.

The Easter message is about hope in this life, and hope for the life to come. Despite the diversity within the New Testament regarding other issues, there is absolute unity on this point: *the crucified Jesus has conquered death, and because he lives, all those who cling to him in faith will also live.* This is the heart of the Easter message. Jesus was raised into God: "Because I live, you also will live" (Jn 14:19). Peter refers to this as "a living hope through the resurrection of Jesus Christ from the dead" (1 Pt 1:3). Paul describes Christian hope this way:

> I want to know Christ and the power of his resurrection and the sharing of his sufferings by becoming like him in his death, if somehow I may attain the resurrection from the dead. Not that I have already obtained this or have already reached the goal; but I press on to make it my own, because Christ Jesus has made me his own. (Phil 3:10-12)

Faith itself is "the assurance of things hoped for, the conviction of things not seen" (Heb 11:1). Indeed, "in hope we were saved" (Rom 8:24).

What is the content of Christian hope? Is it hope for this or that? Hope to avoid hell? Hope to go to heaven? I have a very specific definition of Christian hope:

- Christian hope is hope in God alone and openness to God's future through faith in the risen Lord, Jesus Christ.

In the end, we entrust ourselves to "a faithful Creator" (1 Pt 4:19). We entrust our destiny to God who raised Jesus from the dead. We take the gamble that God, who is faithful in life, will remain faithful beyond death. Because of this, the future is always *God's future.* So why not be open to it? "Through him [Jesus] you have come to trust in God, who raised him from the dead and gave him glory, so that your faith and hope are set on God" (1 Pt 1:21).

Karl Rahner sums it up, "Christianity is faith in the future, in a blessed, infinite future, which is the unveiled presence of the infinite God as our eternal life" (Rahner 1993:616).

11

John and the Church: Backing Off Apocalyptic

Years ago, I wrote my Master's thesis on the Gospel of John. This required spending a year of my life immersed in John's theology. My daughter was born that year and I think her first words as she emerged from the womb were, "In the beginning was the Word, and the Word was with God and the Word was God" (Jn 1:1). At least that's all I remember!

John is certainly the most unique Gospel, quite distinct from Matthew, Mark, and Luke. Objectively, John is an example of late first century *Christ-mysticism,* written for a Christian community in conflict primarily with Judaism, and secondarily, the wider pagan Roman culture.

Theologically, John's agenda is to show that Jesus is the divine Son of God who came down from heaven to bring salvation. Jesus is God incarnate or "the Word made flesh." The core of John's "good news" is *eternal life now.* Jesus says, "I came that they might have life, and have it abundantly" (Jn 10:10). In John, salvation is not a far-off hope; it is a present experience for all those who believe in Jesus. Eternal life is the life of God experienced here and now, not later. This is called "realized eschatology." The life of the age to come has already been realized in the present age. God's coming future has already broken into the world, and the future age of salvation has already begun. Eternal life now! This is the gospel according to John.

John, in other words, is eschatological, but it is not apocalyptic eschatology. Apocalyptic is non-existent in John. There are no visions and dreams. There are no angels flying around and delivering divine messages to prophets. There is no glorious second coming of Christ on the clouds, no earthquakes, floods, or famines. Nation does not rise up against nation or kingdom against kingdom. No celestial signs and wonders, and the heavens are not shaken. There is no millennial kingdom, no beast or false prophet, no Armageddon or Antichrist. John's community was not a group of apocalyptic seers. The church in John was not an apocalyptic church.

John addresses a deeper question, "How does a Christian community survive without the literal, physical presence of Christ?" John's answer is, *the Holy Spirit in the church.* For John, the Spirit *is* the presence of Christ and eternal life. It's all happening now, not in some apocalyptic future. Christ now dwells in the hearts of believers through the Spirit. Those who believe receive eternal life *now* through the power of the Spirit. Christians "abide in Christ" through the Spirit. New truths and revelations come through the Spirit. Christian life is life in the Spirit. Christ is a living Spirit operating in and through the church. This is John's emphasis.

Jesus is no longer with us as a physical, historical person. He has returned to the Father. Now what do we do? John answers this question in "the Farewell Discourses" (chapters 13-17). In these chapters, Jesus talks to his disciples about how to cope with his departure. We gain insight into the nature of the church. Again, John's community is not an apocalyptic group. These Christians plan to be here a while.

Our focus will be John 17. It is a prayer for the unity and mission of the church. Jesus is gathered with his disciples prior to departing to his Father in heaven. He has accomplished his mission on earth and now it is time for the cross. "The hour has come" and soon he will suffer and die (Jn 17:1). Before the tragic drama begins, Jesus prays for his disciples and all future believers. I have divided this essay into three sections: The World, The Church, and The Mission.

The World

> *Righteous Father, the world does not know you, but I know you; and these know that you have sent me.*
>
> *--John 17:25*

The "world" (Greek: *kosmos*) is mentioned approximately eighty times in the Gospel of John. In John 17, "the world" is referred to nineteen times. John views the world as the realm of darkness, ignorance and stubborn unbelief. The world is a force that influences people and pervades the air we breathe. It is an attitude, an orientation to life. The world promotes unbelief. The church is the realm of faith and the world is the realm of unbelief.

The world does not recognize or "know" Jesus as the Messiah. The world refuses to acknowledge "the only true God" and Jesus Christ whom God has sent (17:3). In John, Jesus is "the unrecognized Revealer." He was sent from God, but the world rejected him (1:1-13). The world did not know him and, thus, lies in ignorance and stubborn unbelief. The world persecutes those who believe in Jesus (15:18-19). The world continually resists the gospel. The church and the world are antagonistic toward each other. This is the self-perception of religious groups who see themselves as a persecuted minority surrounded by hostile forces.

In John 17, the church does not belong to the world, yet the church remains in the world (17:14, 16). The church is chosen from out of the world, having received and believed true knowledge about salvation (17:6, 8, 14, 26). The church consists of those who know the "truth" about Jesus. This truth is that God has sent Jesus Christ to be the Savior of the world, and eternal life comes through him.

But doesn't God love the world? John 3:16 says, "For God so loved the world that he gave his only Son, so that everyone who believes in him may not perish but may have eternal life." Here, then, is the paradox: *the world resists the gospel, yet God loves the world and has sent the church into the world.*

John 17 stresses that the church will remain in the world and it is sent into the world (17:11-18). This sending theme is central to John's understanding of the church. The risen Christ, when he appears to his stunned disciples, anoints them with the Spirit and says, "As the Father has sent me, so I send you" (20:21). The church should not retreat from the world. No withdrawal and no apocalyptic flight. The church is to bear witness to the truth of Jesus Christ, so that the world may believe and receive eternal life through him (17:21).

Now let's move on to the heart of John 17, the intercessory prayer of Jesus for the church's protection, unity, and sanctification.

The Church

> *Holy Father, protect them in your name that you have given me, so that they may be one, as we are one.*
>
> *--John 17:11*

The prayer of John 17 is for the protection, unity, and sanctification of the church. By the end of the first century the split between Judaism and Christianity was permanent. Christianity was a new religion fighting for its life. It was imperative to establish a distinct Christian identity. That identity was rooted in Jesus the Christ, crucified, resurrected, and present to the church through the Spirit. Protection, unity, and sanctification were essential to the survival of the church.

Protection. Jesus prayed that the church would be protected from evil. He said, "I am not asking you to take them out of the world, but I ask you to protect them from the evil one" (17:15). This is reminiscent of the Lord's Prayer, "Lead us not into temptation, but deliver us from evil." The "evil one" is the devil, the personification of evil and unbelief. The devil does not stand in the truth but is "the father of lies" (8:44). The devil is "the ruler of this world" but he has no power over Jesus (14:30). Now that Jesus is returning to the Father, he prays that his followers may be protected from evil, from slouching towards unbelief, and from falling away from the truth.

For John and his churches, remaining steadfast in the truth is essential. The truth is the message that Jesus was sent from God, that he is the Messiah, the divine Son of God, and that eternal life comes through him (17:3). Grace and truth come through Jesus Christ (1:17). To know the truth is to be set free (8:32). The Holy Spirit or Comforter is "the spirit of truth" who guides the church into all truth (14:17; 15:26; 16:13). *The church must be maintained in truth.* The concerns here are for spiritual protection and right belief. The church must teach what is true about God and Jesus Christ. John makes it clear that the normative center of the church's faith is God's revelation in Jesus Christ, who is "the way, and the truth, and the life" (14:6).

Unity. Jesus prayed for the unity of the church. He said, "Holy Father, protect them in your name that you have given me, so that they may be one, as we are one" (17:11). Then he prayed, "The glory that you have given me, I have given them, so that they may be one, as we are one, I in them and you in me, that they may become completely one" (17:22-23). This is the theme of the worldwide ecumenical movement, despite Christian diversity.

What did Jesus mean by unity? Was Jesus praying for the centralization of authority? Was he praying that Christians should form one organization with one leader? Did Jesus require unity in doctrine on every issue?

By unity, John 17 is describing *a spiritual union* between the Father, the Son, the Spirit, and the church, a spiritual union based on love. Jesus is not talking about hierarchy or church structures. He is referring to a unity of the Spirit, a unity based on mutual love and fellowship with Christ. This is stated in John 15. Jesus tells Christians to abide in him as he abides in God (15:1-11). The unity for which Jesus prayed is a unity of spirit; the active principle of this unity is love. The world is to know that God loves the church, and the church is to be a fellowship of love (17:23-26). "By this everyone will know that you are my disciples, if you have love for one another" (13:35).

Sanctification. Jesus prayed for the sanctification or holiness of the church. The idea behind this concept is *total dedication.* To be sanctified is to be set apart for a holy purpose. It is a term related not only to piety but to action. Jesus prayed, "Sanctify them in the truth; your word is truth" (17:17). The church is to remain true to its intended purpose: to bear witness to the gospel of Jesus Christ. The church is to be dedicated to this cause. It is God's cause. It is the message about Jesus—his mission and fate. The church is to be established in the truth of the gospel and to not waver. "Your word is truth" means God's word about Jesus Christ.

We have briefly explored John's concept of the world. We have also seen the importance John placed on the protection, the unity, and the sanctification of the church. We now address the mission of the church.

The Mission: Christ-Community-Discipleship

> *As you have sent me into the world, so I have sent them into the world.*
>
> *--John 17:18*

The purpose of the Gospel of John is to provoke faith in Jesus Christ so that people may come to believe that Jesus is the Messiah, the Son of God, and experience eternal life in him (20:31). This is John's missionary agenda. Christians perceive in Jesus Christ the presence of God's eschatological salvation.

Jesus prayed, "As you have sent me into the world, so I have sent them into the world." Jesus also said, "I ask not only on behalf of these, but also on behalf of those who will believe in me through their word" (17:20). The church has an outward mission as well as an inward spiritual life. Apocalyptic communities usually passively await the end of time. They have rejected the world. There is no hope in the world. All hope is aimed at a future salvation. There is also no mission to the world, except to shout, "The end is near!" This is not how John views things. According to John, the church is called to go into the world with the message of *eternal life now.* God's salvation is present here and now, and can be experienced now.

There will be resistance: "In the world you face persecution. But take courage: I have conquered the world" (16:33). Believers are assured that Jesus is with them at all times and in all eras of history; Jesus has already conquered the world and overcome its resistance through the cross and resurrection.

What about the church's mission in a pluralistic, polycentric, secular age? Ours is an age of globalization, multiculturalism, diversity, competing values, science and technology, social fragmentation, professional specialization, urbanization, individualism, materialism, naturalism, and a general breakdown of a dominant cultural ethic. Indeed, there has been a resurgence of religion. But what kind of religion is it? Are not many religious groups angry, reactionary, fundamentalist, violent, and anti-modern? Despite the religious resurgence, Western society remains a scientific, technological, materialistic, secular culture. The church must deal with this in a way that promotes what is good in culture while judging what is not good. We must engage the world *as it is.* We must find common ground and common concerns, while prophetically speaking out against all dehumanizing, anti-God powers.

How can the church present a plausible gospel to the world? In this concluding section, I emphasize Christ, community, and discipleship.

First, the church must never lose experiential contact with its source: Jesus Christ, the incarnate Son of God who brings God's eschatological salvation to the world here and now. As we have seen, this salvation is eternal life for all who believe. This life is nothing less than the life of the age to come experienced in the present age. As Paul Tillich wrote many years ago, "The message of Christianity is not Christianity, but a New Reality" (Tillich 1955:24). This "New Reality" is the message about Jesus Christ and eternal life now.

Second, there must be a serious reconnection with the New Testament understanding of the church as a community. This community is a fellowship of faith and love (*koinonia*). Individual faith is nurtured by the church's faith, and the church's faith needs the contribution of personal faith that each Christian brings. We are the people of God. We live and die as a community of faith grounded in the gospel. In an age when so many people feel adrift and dislocated, without a base or a community, the church offers a sense of belonging and love.

Third, the church must emphasize the revolutionary nature of discipleship. To follow Christ is to be a disciple and to share his fate. We all know what his fate was—the cross. John quotes Jesus as saying,

> Unless a grain of wheat falls into the earth and dies, it remains just a single grain; but if it dies it bears much fruit. Those who love their life will lose it, and those who hate their life in this world will keep it for eternal life." (Jn 12:24-25)

Discipleship is more than attending church once a week and paying our dues. It means dying to self in order to bear fruit for Christ. It means "hating" our life in this world in order to lose ourselves for the sake of the world. This is sharing the fate of Jesus. It reflects his all-out commitment to the will of his Father. There is a powerful story at the end of John's Gospel in which Jesus tests Peter's commitment three times (21:15-23). Then Jesus says,

> Very truly I tell you, when you were younger, you used to fasten your own belt and go wherever you wished. But when you grow old, you will stretch out your hands, and someone else will fasten a belt around you and take you where you do not wish to go." (Jn 21:18)

Clearly, these verses do not imply that the end is near! Rather, they assume that time will continue on, Peter will grow old and will eventually die for his faith; he will go where he does not wish to go. Peter followed Jesus all the way and was eventually executed in Rome.

In summary, the Gospel of John represents "realized eschatology," not apocalyptic eschatology. Eternal life can be experienced now, salvation is now, and God's coming future has already begun. The church is the ongoing incarnation of Christ, who dwells in the church through the Spirit. Though the church looks forward to the Second Coming of Christ (14:1-3), this is not emphasized in John. Rather, the church is a missionary church called to go into the world with the "good news" of salvation through Jesus Christ here and now. The church is the eschatological community of salvation living in the world, witnessing in the world, while resisting the evil in the world.

And this world might continue for quite a while . . .

12

Pentecost

Pentecost (Acts 2) marked the beginning of a new time, a new era of salvation time. Pentecost is eschatological time breaking into ordinary existence. Pentecost is the alarm clock going off and telling people to wake up because it's salvation time!

Peter's Pentecost sermon will be the core of this chapter (Acts 2:14-36). What does Pentecost tell us about the church in relation to the end of the world? Peter's sermon set the agenda for the theology of the early church. It contains the church's *kerygma,* its core gospel. That theology was nothing less than eschatology: the announcement of a new time, the Age of the Spirit.

Prior to his ascension, Jesus ordered the disciples to wait in Jerusalem for the promise of the Spirit. The Spirit would be the sign of the New Age. Jewish theology looked forward to a future time when God would pour out his Spirit upon all flesh. This came to be called "the baptism of the Holy Spirit." In the last days, God's Spirit would infuse all people. This revelation would not be limited to Jews. Thus, Acts begins with Jesus ascending into heaven while the disciples wait and pray in Jerusalem.

Jerusalem? Early Christianity was an urban phenomenon. When Paul went into Europe, he focused on cities. These cities were multicultural hubs. According to Acts, Jerusalem was inhabited by Parthians, Medes, Elamites, people from Mesopotamia, Judea, Cappadocia, Pontus, Asia, Phrygia, Pamphylia, Egypt, Libya, Rome, Crete, and other Arab speaking persons (2:9-11). Pentecost was about a small group of Galileans waking up to the big world and going multicultural. Pentecost paints the church as an international, universal community of salvation breaking free from Judaism and taking the gospel to the world in the power of the Spirit.

Unity and universality are characteristics of the church. Acts describes a movement from Jewish sect to universal church. "Speaking in tongues" is a symbol of this shift. Paul Tillich comments,

> The disciples' ecstatic speaking with tongues was interpreted as the conquest of the disruption of mankind as symbolized in the story of the Tower of Babel. In light of the unity apparent in the story of Pentecost, we must say that there is no Spiritual Community without the ultimate reunion of all the estranged members of mankind. (Tillich 1963:151)

Pentecost forced the Jewish followers of Jesus to begin seeing themselves as "Christians." Hans Kung points out that the church was not born at Pentecost but at Easter. Christian faith is Easter faith, not Pentecost faith. The church existed before Pentecost (Acts 1:15). "But through the giving of the Holy Spirit the community recognized itself and testified to itself as the eschatological community" (Kung 1967:165). Pentecost was the moment the church became conscious of itself as God's chosen community of salvation for the last days. It was an eschatological church announcing salvation in Christ and the nearness of the end.

Pentecost also forced the followers of Jesus into mission. This mission would include "all who are far away, all whom the Lord our God calls to him" (2:39). This was a movement from exclusiveness to inclusiveness. We might call it "catholicity," meaning comprehensiveness as contrasted with sectarian. The church was to become a comprehensive and inclusive community of faith for all people, not a sect for the select few. The catholic impulse asks, "How many can we include?" not "Whom shall we exclude?" It would take some time for the apostles to live into this vision, but the plan is set forth in Acts 1:8,

> But you will receive power when the Holy Spirit has come upon you; and you will be my witnesses in Jerusalem, in all Judea and Samaria, and to the ends of the earth.

Acts follows this agenda of expansion. The Pentecost picture of the church is that of an eschatological community of salvation grounded in Jesus Christ and marked by *unity, universality, and catholicity.* This brings us to Peter's sermon.

Peter's Pentecost Sermon: Acts 2:14-36

No one knows precisely what happened that day. The Pentecost story has been embellished and dramatized by Luke. We can be confident, however, as to what happened *theologically.* On that day "the Jesus movement" became a self-conscious church. The separation from Judaism began with an eschatological message centered on Jesus of Nazareth, the crucified Messiah who had been raised from the dead and exalted to heaven.

Luke uses a prophetic passage from Joel referring to the last days. Joel predicted a future "day of the Lord" when God's Spirit would be poured out universally on all men and women, and they would prophesy or speak the word of the Lord. This would be a populist movement of the Spirit accompanied by apocalyptic signs and wonders (Joel 2:28-32). The message of salvation would go to all those willing to accept it, for "everyone who calls upon the name of the Lord shall be saved." For those who refused the message, there would be judgment. Here we see the apocalyptic aroma of the early church with an emphasis on "the last days." The messianic age of salvation is here.

Two features should be noted: *continuity and fulfillment*. The first Christians were Jews who stressed the continuity between God's revelation to ancient Israel and God's revelation through Jesus of Nazareth. They were convinced that Jesus fulfilled the promises made to Israel. These Jewish Christians reinterpreted the Old Testament in light of the Christ-event. Luke draws from Joel and the Psalms to support the view that the Day of the Lord has arrived, the promise of the Spirit is being fulfilled, and the Messiah was to suffer, die, and be raised from the dead. Acts shows how Christians began to read the scriptures in light of their experience of Jesus Christ.

Judaism as a whole did not accept the new interpretation of its scriptures. The Christian approach was innovative to the point of being heresy. A split was inevitable. Christian experience led the way in the reinterpretation of the Old Testament. Experience led to the reinterpretation of the texts.

Peter's sermon shows how the early church used the Old Testament. An important hermeneutical principle is revealed: *we interpret the scriptures through the lens of our own experience*. Those first Jewish Christians had been encountered by the risen Lord, and this changed the way they understood the scriptures. They took liberties with the ancient texts. What mattered most was the experience of Jesus as Lord, next came the reinterpretation of Old Testament prophecies. Peter used the Old Testament to confirm the experience of Jesus as Lord.

Luke had already made this point in the post-resurrection story of the walk to Emmaus (Lk 24:13-35). In that story the risen Christ appears in disguise and points the disciples to the scriptures: "Then beginning with Moses and the prophets, he interpreted to them the things about himself in all the scriptures" (Lk 24:27). The early Christian community developed a set of proof-texts used in missionary preaching to substantiate the claim that Jesus was the long-expected Messiah. The proof-texts were not convincing to most Jews, though some were won over. These texts were recycled again and again throughout church history and used in Christian polemics against Judaism. The message was clear: Christianity is in direct continuity with God's revelation to ancient Israel, and Jesus the Messiah fulfills God's promises to Israel.

The next feature of Peter's sermon is *foreknowledge*. The idea of a crucified Messiah was offensive to Jews, but the Christian gospel proclaimed that God foresaw everything. God planned everything just as it happened, including the death of Jesus. Jesus was "a man attested to you by God with deeds of power, wonders, and signs that God did through him among you, as you yourselves know"; he was delivered up to death "according to the definite plan and foreknowledge of God" (2:22-23). Having been raised from the dead, Jesus was exalted to heaven and now reigns as Lord. Peter concludes by saying,

> Therefore let the entire house of Israel know with certainty that God has made him both Lord and Messiah, this Jesus whom you crucified. (Acts 2:36)

To foreknowledge we may add *exaltation*. This is exaltation Christology, not incarnation Christology. Peter said, "Being therefore exalted at the right hand of God, and having received from the Father the promise of the Holy Spirit, he has poured out this that you both see and hear" (2:33). This early form of Christology viewed Jesus as a human being called by God to be the Messiah and exalted to heaven as Lord. According to this Christology, Jesus is not a God-Man. He did not come down from heaven (as in the Gospel of John). Rather, he was a man whom God called to be the Messiah. He was crucified, raised from the dead and exalted into heaven. The pouring out of the Spirit was the sign of his Lordship. In Acts, exaltation Christology dominates.

The core message is,

- Jesus is the Messiah, crucified, risen from the dead, exalted to heaven, and he now reigns as Lord. The gift of the Holy Spirit is the eschatological sign of his Lordship and the beginning of the New Age of salvation.

The last segment of Peter's sermon is the *appeal*, "Repent, and be baptized every one of you in the name of Jesus Christ so that your sins may be forgiven; and you will receive the Holy Spirit" (2:38). This is the call to enter the eschatological community of salvation, the church. The initiation rite is baptism by water, symbolizing repentance, cleansing from sin, and the infilling of the Spirit. Baptism is an eschatological event by which a person transfers from the old age to the new age, from the old life of sin to the kingdom of God. According to Acts, three thousand persons were baptized that day (2:41).

These elements constitute early Christian preaching and can be seen in Peter's sermon at Pentecost:

- Continuity and fulfillment
- God's foreknowledge
- The death and resurrection of Jesus the Christ
- Exaltation Christology
- Baptism and the gift of the Spirit
- Eschatological salvation in a universal church

A Church in the Power of the Spirit?

An eschatological church? A church in the power of the Spirit?

The church is a sinful church always in need of reform. The Pentecost story brings us back to our roots. It reminds us what the church is called to be and do. Pentecost is about Christian identity.

First, Pentecost was not an ordinary experience. It was an ecstatic experience generated by the Holy Spirit. Ecstasy comes from the Greek word meaning "to stand outside oneself." Pentecost was literally an "outstanding" experience in that the apostles were overtaken by the power of the Spirit and were infused with uncommon gifts and uncommon influence. Genuine spiritual ecstasy is at the heart of Christian experience. This is the true "baptism of the Spirit," the result of which is the effective proclamation of the gospel.

The church is the result of the creative impact of the Spirit. It is by the Spirit that the church recognizes Jesus as the Christ. Apart from the Spirit, no one recognizes Jesus as the Christ. "Only Spirit can discern Spirit" (Tillich 1963:150; cf. 1 Cor 2:6-16). Despite all rational attempts to convince people that Jesus is the Christ, only the Spirit can move the human heart and mind to say yes to the gospel. Otherwise, Christian proclamation is lifeless polemics and ineffective arguments.

Second, the living Christ is present in the church through the Spirit. Jesus was present to those first disciples through the Spirit. Jesus communicated with them through the Spirit. Jesus was present in their preaching through the Spirit. They were not merely proclaiming a past event; they were proclaiming a living Lord who was alive through the Spirit. Later, Paul wrote, "Now the Lord is the Spirit, and where the Spirit of the Lord is, there is freedom" (2 Cor 3:17). This is perhaps the best summary of Pentecost itself.

The living Lord is present now in the church in word, sacrament, and service. The Spirit is speaking now to the church. What is it saying? *"Preach Christ and invite people into the life of the eschatological age of salvation."*

In summary, an overemphasis on apocalyptic eschatology denies the living presence of the Lord in the church and the world today. It is escapist in attitude and pessimistic in tone. The church is not a doomsday community based on doomsday theology. Christianity is a message of salvation *now* because the New Age is already here. The kingdom is already present, although not in its fullness. Apocalypticism denies the kingdom as a present reality in order to stress the future kingdom.

On the other hand, liberal Christianity too easily loses itself in the world while ignoring the eschatological message of the coming kingdom. The Spirit is certainly at work in every endeavor to improve society. The Spirit is present in every social movement for justice, freedom, liberation, and human dignity. But the church is not a social services agency. According to Acts, it is the eschatological community of salvation that has a horizon beyond this world. The church must always resist secular utopianism as a pseudo-religion, a form of misdirected eschatology. The Spirit calls the church to preach Christ and invite people into the life of God's coming kingdom.

We have seen that the church recognizes in Jesus the saving presence of the Christ, the universal Savior. The church is marked by unity, universality, catholicity, and a mission to the world. It is a missionary church that proclaims God's coming future in the power of the Spirit.

13

Rescue from Orion?

When I was a child I was told that Jesus would literally return to earth via the constellation Orion. He would travel through outer space, past galaxies and stars. He would literally appear in the sky overhead and descend to earth surrounded by angels. The graves would open and the dead would be raised. The wicked would be slain by "the brightness of his coming."

The glorious appearing of Jesus would be preceded by dark days, including plagues, earthquakes, wars, famines, persecution, death and destruction. It would be a terrible time of chaos and bloodshed. But God's "remnant people" would be saved at last. Then we would be lifted up in the air and go to heaven with Jesus.

Are Christians required to believe in the literal return of Christ, a literal rescue from outer space? To reject the literal second coming of Christ does not mean rejecting eschatological hope. It means rejecting a literal interpretation of apocalyptic language and symbols.

I have emphasized that Jesus and the early Christians lived in an apocalyptic world saturated with apocalyptic mythology.

Apocalyptic must be reinterpreted or demythologized in order to preserve its essential message. We should be more interested in eschatological promise than in apocalyptic information.

This chapter addresses the second coming of Christ as described by Paul in First Thessalonians.

The New Testament uses the Greek word *parousia* to refer to Christ's coming in glory. Literally, it means "presence" or "arrival." We could call it "Christ's coming presence" (Moltmann 1996:25). Jesus was present in the flesh during his earthly life. He is present now through the Holy Spirit. But *parousia* is used only to refer to his future coming in power and glory at the end of time. The coming of Christ is understood as a literal event that will take place soon. The Apostles' Creed states, "He will come again to judge the living and dead." This is advent hope, "advent" being the Latin translation of *parousia.*

Christians are Advent people who are waiting for the final arrival of Christ in glory. We believe God has a plan for history, and God will bring history to a conclusion through Jesus Christ. Should we look for a literal return of Christ on the clouds or interpret the coming of Christ another way? What, in other words, is *permanently valid and eternally decisive* in advent hope? We begin with Paul's apocalyptic horizon in First Thessalonians.

Paul's Apocalyptic Horizon

Paul faced the daunting task of proclaiming an eschatological message to a pagan culture. He had to convince the Greco-Roman world that Jesus was coming soon. This included God's wrath and the final judgment. Some people believed him and they became Christians. They were the "chosen." Paul, driven by a sense of urgency, believed time was running down and the end was near. He wanted to save as many people as possible before it was too late. He was propelled by his belief in the imminent return of Christ. We find a summary of Paul's missionary preaching in First Thessalonians,

> For the people of those regions report about us what kind of welcome we had among you, and how you turned to God from idols, to serve a living and true God, and to wait for his Son from heaven, whom he raised from the dead—Jesus, who rescues us from the wrath that is coming. (1 Thess 1:9-10)

Turning from idols, worshiping the true God, faith in Christ who was raised from the dead, hope in the coming of Christ and salvation from the wrath to come—this is an eschatological message.

A few persons in Thessalonica received Paul's message as God's word, "in power and in the Holy Spirit and with full conviction" (1:5). It was more than a human message; it was a convicting message that took root in people's hearts and resulted in faith, hope, and love. All in all, Paul's preaching in Thessalonica was successful. A Christian community of Gentile converts was born. This community was committed to a love grounded in the gospel of Christ and hope in his soon coming,

> May the Lord make you increase and abound in love for one another and for all . . . may he so strengthen your hearts in holiness that you may be blameless before our God and Father at the coming of our Lord Jesus Christ with all his saints. (1 Thess 3:12-13)

The early Pauline churches viewed themselves as communities of salvation awaiting the end of the world and the coming of Christ in glory. They had been chosen out of the world by God for salvation (1:4). They were "children of light and children of the day" in the midst of a pagan culture immersed in idolatry and sin (5:5). They were called to live lives worthy of God and God's kingdom (2:12). They were called to nothing less than holiness or sanctification (4:2-8). The highest form of this holiness was *love*. All of Paul's advice regarding Christian ethics was generated by his belief in the end of the world. The message is, *"Be holy because there isn't much time left. Jesus is coming soon! There will be salvation for those who believe and live holy lives, but wrath for nonbelievers and sinners."*

Paul embraced an apocalyptic worldview based on a dualistic understanding of history. There are two ages: the present evil age and the age to come. Believers live in the present evil age, but soon Jesus will come to rescue them and inaugurate the age to come. Paul did not stress reforming the world. He never initiated social programs to improve society. Rather, history is getting bad and things will get worse until Jesus appears to bring in the New Age.

The church, in Paul's view, is the eschatological community of salvation waiting for Jesus to arrive in glory and power. This is classic Jewish apocalyptic with a Christian twist. Bart Ehrman states, "Thus, in its simplest terms, Paul's proclamation was designed to transform the Thessalonian pagans into Jewish apocalypticists, who believed that Jesus was the key to the end of the world" (Ehrman 2000:282).

Jesus also taught the two ages. One example is his parable of the weeds growing among the wheat (Matt 13:24-30). Weeds and wheat must grow together until the final judgment when God separates them. The present age is characterized by good and evil existing side by side until the coming of the Son of Man in glory and the final day of reckoning. He will inaugurate the New Age, God's kingdom. Jesus said,

> Just as the weeds are collected and burned up with fire, so will it be at the end of the age. The Son of Man will send his angels, and they will collect out of his kingdom all causes of sin and all evildoers, and they will throw them into the furnace of fire, where there will be weeping and gnashing of teeth. (Matt 13:40-42)

Paul inherited this apocalyptic tradition and preached it to the Gentiles. He proclaimed divine rescue from the present evil age. He believed in the literal coming of Christ and the establishment of the age to come.

What are Christians supposed to do while they wait? They should live holy lives. They should avoid evil and sexual immorality and drunkenness. They should remain sober and vigilant. In the midst of idolatry, they are to serve the living God. They should do honest labor and not be lazy. They should lead quiet lives. God will soon deal with the Roman Empire, wait for salvation from God. It won't be long. There is nothing in First Thessalonians about Christians working to change *the system*. With the end of the world bearing down on them, *the system* would soon be crushed by God, or so they believed.

The Thessalonians didn't seem concerned about social justice issues. They were more interested in the fate their deceased loved ones. Paul addressed this issue in 1 Thessalonians 4:13-18. Dispensationalists who teach the Rapture view this passage as a description of the Rapture. This is erroneous, and I will address dispensationalism and the Rapture in a later chapter (see Chapter Nineteen).

The Coming of the Lord

We will begin with 1 Thessalonians 4:13-15:

> But we do not want you to be uninformed, brothers and sisters, about those who have died, so that you may not grieve as others do who have no hope. For since we believe that Jesus died and rose again, even so, through Jesus, God will bring with him those who have died. For this we declare to you by the word of the Lord, that we who are alive, who are left until the coming of the Lord, will by no means precede those who have died. (1 Thess 4:13-15)

First we hear Paul's pastoral concern for the Thessalonians. What is the issue? It is grief. Certain persons in this congregation are grieving and want to know if there is a future for their deceased loved ones. They seem to think that Jesus will return to earth, rescue the believers who are alive, and forget the dead. Is Christ the Lord of the dead as well as the living? Do the dead also have an eternal destiny in God? The main issue is the relationship between the Lord and the dead.

Is there a future for the dead? Paul says yes. Christ is the Lord of the dead as well as the living (see Chapter Eighteen). Christians need not sorrow as those who have no hope. They can be assured that their deceased loved ones who have died "in Christ" are safe in God's hands and will be resurrected, just as Christ was raised from the dead. H. K. McArthur comments, "Christians are comforted about their dead, not with the promise that at death they enter into God's presence, but rather with the hope of the Parousia, which is to occur in that generation" (1962:659). Paul doesn't say, "Don't worry about the dead; they are already with the Lord in heaven." Instead he says, "Don't worry about the dead. Jesus is coming soon and he will resurrect them."

We have seen that the resurrection is an apocalyptic idea related to theodicy (see Chapter Ten). At the resurrection, God will vindicate those who have suffered injustice, persecution, and martyrdom. The resurrection answers the question about the fate of the dead and God's justice at the end of time.

Let's move on now to the rest of the passage,

> For the Lord himself, with a cry of command, with the archangel's call and with the sound of God's trumpet, will descend from heaven, and the dead in Christ will rise first. Then we who are alive, who are left, will be caught up in the clouds together with them to meet the Lord in the air; and so we will be with the Lord forever. Therefore, encourage one another with these words. (1 Thess 4:16-18)

Paul portrays the *parousia* as a dramatic, public event that will soon take place. Christ appears as a transcendent Savior who brings an ultimate resolution to history. This is the old Jewish hope in the coming of the Messiah, now cast in cosmic terms with a Christian twist. Jesus comes to finish what he began. God's people have given up hope in reforming history. They look outside of history for salvation: *a supernatural invasion from on high.* They are a small band of true believers united in hope that God will soon act to vindicate them and vanquish the wicked.

Paul lived in close proximity to Jewish apocalyptic thought and the Jewish hope in the coming of "the son of man" (Dan 7:13-14). This was the hope of the early church. Jewish Christians did not expect a political Messiah like David. Jesus would soon be revealed as the transcendent Savior in power and glory to set up God's kingdom. We can trace this belief back to Jesus:

> Then the sign of the Son of Man will appear in heaven, and then all the tribes of the earth will mourn, and they will see the Son of Man coming on the clouds of heaven with power and great glory. And he will send out his angels with a loud trumpet call, and they will gather his elect from the four winds, from one end of heaven to the other. (Matt 24:30-31)

In 1Thessalonians 4:13-18, Paul is repeating the Christian hope in the coming of the Son of Man in glory. The ideas of the coming of the Son of Man, the gathering of God's elect, the resurrection of the righteous, and the destruction of wicked, find their roots in Jewish apocalyptic. The coming of Christ will be like the state visit of a ruler, preceded by a retinue of lesser dignitaries, the blowing of trumpets, the fanfare, the homage, and the gaudy display of political and military might. Everyone is in awe, everyone bows and stares, everyone shows proper obeisance.

As long as those first Christians lived with a sense of the

imminent end of all things, the apocalyptic message was effective. As long as people were convinced that Jesus was coming soon—in their lifetime—the message stirred up passion and moral transformation. Hope in Christ's coming should motivate people to live holy lives as they wait for their final deliverance.

For example, Paul believed in the literal wrath of God poured out on earth on "the day of the Lord" (5:2). He preached that Jesus saves people from "the wrath that is coming" (1:10). Jews who rejected Christ have already been overtaken by "God's wrath" and, apparently, are lost (2:16). Paul said, "The Lord is an avenger" (4:6). The "day of the Lord" will come unexpectedly like a thief in the night and will bring "sudden destruction" on the wicked (5:3). But Christians are aware of "the times and the seasons" (5:1). They are "children of light and children of the day," whereas the unbelieving world is in darkness and doomed to destruction. God has not destined Christians for wrath but for salvation in Jesus Christ (5:9-10).

Paul concludes his appeal with the benediction,

> May the God of peace himself sanctify you entirely; and may your spirit and soul and body be kept sound and blameless at the coming of our Lord Jesus Christ. (1 Thess 5:23)

What Does the Coming of Christ Mean Today?

Apocalyptic hope recycles through Christian history. Apocalyptic fervor usually arises during periods of social breakdown, moral decay, international conflicts, economic insecurity, national crises, and political oppression. Yet history has continued for centuries. Apocalyptic predictions have been discredited again and again. Christian history is littered with the wreckage of apocalyptic dreams that never came true. The Christians in Thessalonica cherished Advent hope, but Jesus never came to rescue them. They all died, including Paul. Was it all in vain? Millions of Christians since then have longed for "rescue from Orion," but deliverance has not come.

Haven't we had enough of apocalyptic predictions and doomsday prophets? In fact, shouldn't we repudiate apocalyptic as mythological nonsense? Is apocalyptic necessary for Christians?

As I have stressed throughout this book, we cannot eliminate apocalyptic; it must be reinterpreted or demythologized. Apocalyptic hope is part of the Christian tradition, and apocalyptic literature is in the Bible. It is not a major part of the Bible, but it is there and it has exerted tremendous influence over the centuries. We must ask: *What is permanently valid and eternally decisive in Advent hope?* If we can no longer believe in a literal rescue from Orion, what does the coming of Christ mean?

First, it means no earthly utopia. The kingdom of God is an act of God, not the result of human works. In the end, God will finish what God has begun. The coming of Christ is not precipitated by social revolution or violence in order to "hasten the day." We must reject all fanaticism that uses violence, terrorism, and murder in order to speed up the end. We must also reject secular ideologies that profess to create the kingdom on earth, such as communism, socialism, fascism, democratic nationalism, and hyper-patriotism. God's kingdom alone will stand at the end of time, not the kingdoms of the world.

Second, no escapism. The coming of Christ is not an excuse for Christians to retreat from society, to form an exclusive sect, and to ignore the problems of the world. Futurology must be countered with prophetic action. Jesus believed in the soon-coming kingdom, but he spoke the prophetic word and did prophetic deeds. The coming future of God does not mean abandoning the present. It is a call, like Paul said, to active holiness that calls for repentance and transformation. Hans Kung writes, "The future is God's call to the present. Life is now to be shaped in the light of the absolute future" (Kung 1976:222).

Third, Christ is always on the way. No one knows the day or the hour of the Lord's coming. But one thing is certain: the coming Christ is always on the way. God's *eschaton* is moving towards us. We are not looking for apocalyptic information but for eschatological hope. This world is finite and someday it will end. Then what? *God.* We do not know how the end will come. We do not know anything about future events. But we know the future belongs to God, and God's future is bearing down on us. The kingdom is always coming.

Finally, Christ is Lord of the dead as well as the living. This is why we can die in peace and in hope. In the end, *there is God.* In the end, there is not emptiness or meaninglessness or futility, *there is God.* God is ultimately sovereign and will have the final word in history and the final say regarding human destiny. As Paul said, "Therefore, encourage one another with these words" (1 Thess 4:18).

14

Paul and Israel: Redefining the People of God

O the depth of the riches and wisdom and knowledge of God! How unsearchable are his judgments and how inscrutable his ways!

--*Romans 11:33*

This reflection is an appraisal of Paul's interpretation of Israel and the church. The relation of Israel and the church is an important theme in Christian eschatology, and it was central to Paul's mission and passion.

Paul can be difficult to understand, but we can't deny his influence on Christian theology. Prior to his conversion, Paul was a Pharisee and a zealous Jewish traditionalist. He was a "Hebrew born of Hebrews," a true blue Israelite, a member of the tribe of Benjamin, and a persecutor of the church (Phil 3:4-6). Paul assumed that the Jews held special status in God's eyes. Salvation for the world, in his view, came through Israel. He wrote, "I advanced in Judaism beyond many of my people of the same age, for I was far more zealous for the traditions of my ancestors" (Gal 1:14).

Paul's Jewish heritage was the determining center of his life until he met Jesus Christ. His conversion changed everything. On the road to Damascus he received a startling vision of the living Christ and heard the voice of Jesus speaking to him. The revelation of Christ broke through Paul's consciousness (Gal 1:11-12). Paul was forced to go back and reinterpret God's revelation to Israel in light of Jesus Christ. He embarked on a lifelong study of the Jewish scriptures from an entirely new point of view. Christ became the center of Paul's mind and heart,

> I regard everything as loss because of the surpassing knowledge of knowing Christ Jesus my Lord. For his sake I have suffered the loss of all things, and I regard them as rubbish, in order that I may gain Christ and be found in him. (Phil 3:8-9)

Rubbish? Paul reviewed his life as a Pharisee, his pride in his Jewish lineage, and his strict obedience to the Torah. He concluded it was "rubbish." He had found a new love: Jesus Christ. Because of this, *Paul redefined Israel.* In light of Jesus Christ and from the perspective of his own conversion and call, Paul looked back and redefined Israel. This required a new and radical reinterpretation of salvation history.

Before moving forward, the topic of Paul and Israel is difficult and has created divisions in contemporary Christianity. Dispensationalism, for example, makes a distinction between Israel and the church. God has two distinct plans, we are told, one for Israel and one for Christians. At the Rapture, the church will be taken up to heaven and removed from history; then God will refocus his attention on national, literal Israel. Dispensationalists assume that the Old Testament prophecies regarding Israel will be literally fulfilled. Indeed, the millennium, according to dispensationalism, is a Jewish kingdom centered in Jerusalem with a literal temple and literal blood sacrifices carried out by literal priests. I discuss dispensationalism in a later chapter (see Chapter Twenty). Paul, I believe, would be shocked at dispensational theology.

We will now address Paul's problem with Israel.

Paul's Problem

> *I glorify my ministry in order to make my own people jealous, and thus save some of them.*
>
> --*Romans 11:13-14*

Paul carried a burden in his heart for Israelites "according to the flesh." To the Christians in Rome he wrote, "I have great sorrow and unceasing anguish in my heart" (Rom 9:2). Paul considered the Jews "my own people" (Rom 9:3; 11:14). He identified with ethnic Israel. This was his physical lineage, and this is what Paul meant by the phrase "according to the flesh." He was talking about biological descent and ethnic lineage: the Jews (Israel) as an ethnic, national entity; the Jews as physical descendents of Abraham. These are the ones Paul was concerned about: "My heart's desire and prayer to God for them is that they may be saved" (Rom 10:1).

God chose Israel and gave Israel "the adoption, the glory, the covenants, the giving of the law, the worship, and the promises" (Rom 9:4). The Messiah was to come through Israel. In fact, in Paul's view the Jews are still beloved by God (Rom 11:28). Despite these advantages, the Jews rejected Christ. Only a minority of Jews accepted Jesus of Nazareth as the Messiah.

To make matters more complicated, Paul was called to be an apostle to the Gentiles. Now he had a problem on his hands. If both Jews and Gentiles are saved by faith in Christ, and the church is the new community of salvation, then what about literal Israel? Paul could not deny God's revelation through Israel in the past, but he certainly could not deny God's ultimate revelation through Jesus Christ and the fact that most Jews did not believe.

Paul viewed the church as the new eschatological community of the last days. God had created a new covenant community founded on the life, death, and resurrection of his Son, Jesus Christ. So, what about Israel? Paul redefined Israel. He redefined the people of God.

Paul wrestled with the continuing validity of Israel in God's purpose. He embarked on a theological journey of reinterpretation based on distinctions between literal Israel (the Jews) and spiritual Israel (the church),

Natural Israel—Spiritual Israel
Physical Descendents of Abraham—Spiritual Descendents of Abraham
Israel according to the flesh—Israel according to the promise
Israel as a nation—Israel as a "faithful remnant"

Will the Real Jew Please Stand Up?

For not all Israelites truly belong to Israel.

--Romans 9:6

Paul argued with his fellow Jews throughout the Greco-Roman world. Most Jews rejected his message, some violently. A few Jews believed, but only a few. On the whole, Paul's missionary preaching to Jews was a failure in terms of numbers of converts. But he viewed Jewish Christians as a "faithful remnant." His interpretation of Israel is based on "remnant theology."

Remnant theology is the belief that God has a group of true believers and true worshipers embedded in "the chosen people." This is a group of the elect within the larger group. Israel as a nation was never totally obedient to God. The Old Testament is the history of Israel's failure and God's faithfulness to his covenant with Israel. In spite of the failure of Israel as a whole, there existed within Israel a faithful remnant that embodied fidelity. Paul alludes to this in his reference to Elijah (Rom 11:2-4). Despite the dark times of Elijah, God had preserved a remnant of faithful Israelites. Paul concludes, "So too at the present time there is a remnant chosen by grace" (Rom 11:5). This argument is the key to Paul's reinterpretation of Israel. He viewed *Jewish Christians* as the faithful remnant "chosen by grace." F. F. Bruce states, "Even so, there remained a chosen remnant of Jewish believers in Christ, and as in earlier days so now it was in the faithful remnant that the hope of the people's future was embodied" (Bruce 1977:333).

In Romans 9:6-7 Paul states, "For not all Israelites truly belong to Israel, and not all of Abraham's children are his true descendents." These verses provide an interpretive key in understanding Paul and Israel. Paul makes a distinction between natural Israel and "true Israelites," that is, Jewish believers in Christ. Jewish Christians embody true Israel and are the legitimate children of Abraham.

Paul said something similar in Romans 2:28-29,

> For a person is not a Jew who is one outwardly, nor is true circumcision something external and physical. Rather, a person is a Jew who is one inwardly, and real circumcision is a matter of the heart—it is spiritual and not literal.

By redefining Israel, Paul redefined "the true Jew" as a person who believed in Jesus Christ and lived according to the Spirit, not according to the flesh. Here we see the movement from literal Israel to spiritual Israel, from physical descent to spiritual descent, from natural, ethnic Israel to the spiritual community of the church. Paul viewed the church as supplanting literal Israel. To him, the church was the new people of God.

All Israel will be Saved?

And so all Israel will be saved . . .

--Romans 11:26

Technically, not all Israel will be saved. A remnant will be saved, a remnant "chosen by grace." I find no place in Paul where he says that *Israel as a people according to the flesh* will be saved.

Paul was painfully aware that most Jews were lost. I, personally, disagree with him on this point, but I believe this is what Paul taught. He was concerned that unbelieving Jews were lost because of their unbelief. He writes that "a hardening has come upon part of Israel" (Rom 11:25). Natural, literal Israel rejected the gospel. Yet Paul took the long view of things. He looked down the road and saw a miracle occurring in the future. When the full number of Gentiles has come to faith in Christ, then there will be a remnant of Jews who also believe—*but not the whole nation Israel!* Paul did not say exactly when or how this would happen. It's a mystery (Rom 11:25). But this remnant of believing Jews will be saved the same way all people are saved: through faith in Jesus Christ. These believing Jews will be grafted back onto the "olive tree" (Rom 11:17-24) and will join other "true Israelites" (Jewish and Gentile Christians).

In Romans 11:13-14, Paul writes, "Now I am speaking to you Gentiles. Inasmuch as I am an apostle to the Gentiles, I glorify my ministry in order to make my own people jealous, and thus save some of them." Paul never envisioned all Jews being saved. Only the faithful remnant would be saved. He wanted to save some of them.

It's important to note what Paul does not say. He does not say that literal Israel will be saved. He does not say that every Jew on earth will be saved simply for being Jewish. He does not say that the Old Testament prophecies regarding Israel will be literally fulfilled. He does not say that the Rapture will remove the church from history and then the Jews will come to faith in Christ. None of these positions can be substantiated by reference to Paul.

In light of Jesus Christ and the gospel, in light of Paul's conversion and call, in light of the church as the new community of the last days, literal Israel was superfluous. Salvation history had reached a turning point in Christ. Paul was living on the other side of the new revelation. Everything had changed. There was no going back and time was running out.

Paul held an exclusive view of salvation: *salvation through faith in Christ alone*. Particularism runs through every letter that Paul wrote. God saves the world through a particular Savior. God justifies the ungodly through a particular event: the cross and resurrection. God's people form a particular community of salvation: the church. Paul dragged the particularism of Judaism into Christianity. His Jewish particularism never disappeared entirely. His gospel was international, but Paul did not preach universalism. To him, the gospel "is the power of God for salvation to everyone who has faith, to the Jew first and also to the Greek" (Rom 1:16). Those who do not have faith are, apparently, not called and are lost.

It is easy to understand why Paul's theology is offensive to Jews. Paul's particularism also creates problems in our pluralistic age in which we have achieved a certain level of parity between the world's religions. We are more inclined toward dialogue and to finding points of commonality between religions. Nevertheless, the key to understanding the mind of Paul is to let Paul be himself. Paul represents an exclusive view of salvation. I do not believe Paul viewed the non-Christian religions as "valid paths to the Absolute." To him, Jesus Christ was the final revelation of God, the universal Savior, and salvation comes only through faith in Christ.

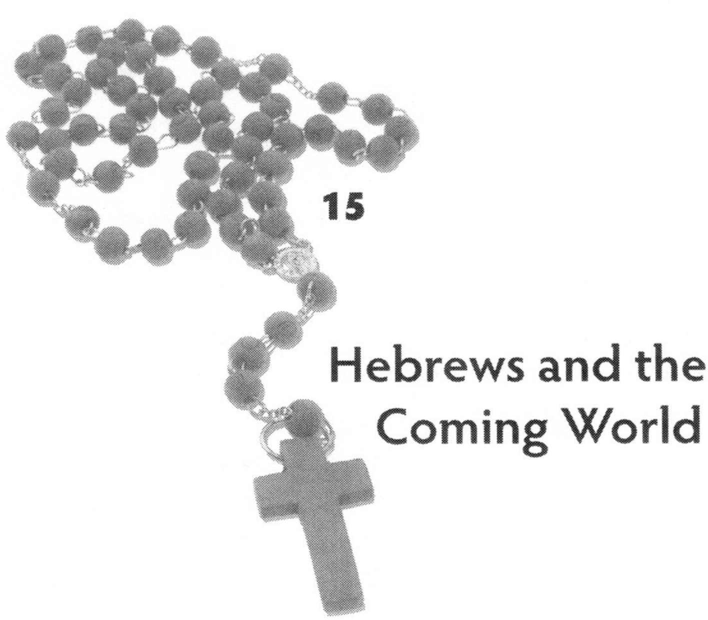

15

Hebrews and the Coming World

The letter to the Hebrews is eschatology minus apocalyptic intrigue. There is no attempt to map out the events leading to the end of the world. There are no calculations about times and seasons. There is no mythological drama or cryptic numbers to decipher. The second coming of Christ and the final judgment are affirmed, but there is no doomsday theology.

Hebrews is entirely eschatological, and Jesus Christ is portrayed as our eschatological mediator and great high priest. God's coming future is the backdrop of the entire letter. Hebrews is about "the coming world" (2:5). Christians have tasted "the powers of the age to come" (6:5). They are living "in these last days" (1:2). Clearly, the ages have shifted and a new time has begun. Christians must persevere in faith and hope up to the end, for "faith is the assurance of things hoped for, the conviction of things not seen" (11:1).

Hope is not wishful thinking, as if to say, "I hope I get a better job" or "I hope my kids are healthy and happy." Hope means *eschatological hope*. It is rock solid confidence in the God who can be trusted to keep his promises, the God of Jesus Christ. This is the God of history who is moving history to a conclusion in the kingdom of God: "Therefore, since we are receiving a kingdom that cannot be shaken, let us give thanks . . ." (12:28). In light of God's faithfulness, Christians should not become sluggish but should imitate those "who through faith and patience inherit the promises" (6:12).

We do not know who wrote Hebrews, nor when the letter was written, or to whom. It seems likely the recipients were Gentile converts who were in danger of abandoning faith in Christ and who needed to be grounded in the faith.

Hebrews reads like a sermon or an exhortation (13:22). Its primary aim is to encourage Christians to keep the faith by reminding them of God's coming future. There is also a polemical purpose. Hebrews is Christian polemic written to justify Christianity in a world that rejects it or simply ignores it as an aberration. In the first century A.D. Christianity was a very small religious sect fighting for its life in a hostile world. Christianity was competing with paganism and polytheism, and it was in conflict with Judaism, a much larger and more established religion.

The central metaphor of Hebrews is *pilgrimage*. Pilgrimage implies a journey from here to there, from this world to the next, from present troubles to "rest" (4:1-11). Hebrews assumes that history may go on for a while longer, but the end is certain because God is faithful and God will keep his promises. The final aim of all things is "the heavenly Jerusalem," the city of the living God (12:22).

Christian life is a pilgrimage grounded in the promises of God and the faithful example of Jesus. Christians are "strangers and foreigners on the earth," seeking an eternal homeland, "a better country" (11:13-16). They must look continually to Jesus, who is "the pioneer and perfecter of our faith" (12:2). Suffering must be patiently endured, "For here we have no lasting city, but we are looking for a city that is to come" (13:14).

I have divided this chapter into three parts:

- Promise and Fulfillment
- Pilgrimage and Perseverance
- Eschatological Rest

Promise and Fulfillment

> *But Jesus has now obtained a more excellent ministry, and to that degree he is the mediator of a better covenant, which has been enacted through better promises.*
>
> *--Hebrews 8:6*

Something new and better has occurred and has replaced what was old and inferior. The author of Hebrews writes with a comprehensive knowledge of Judaism and the Old Testament. He is convinced that Christianity is superior to Judaism because Jesus Christ is the fulfillment of Judaism and the Jewish law. The theme is *promise and fulfillment*. Christ has fulfilled the promises of God to Israel. A new time has begun, the time of fulfillment, the time of the "new covenant." What is old is obsolete and passing away (8:13).

Hebrews highlights the issue of Christian identity. The first Christians were Jews who believed Jesus was the Messiah. Judaism rejected this message and the gospel of Christ was taken to the Gentiles. Hebrews was written in the heat of the battle with Judaism. Though not anti-Semitic, Hebrews is definitely anti-Judaism. It asserts that Christianity is superior to Judaism because Christ himself is superior. Thus, the author of Hebrews writes about continuity and superiority (Ehrman 2000). There is continuity between the Jewish tradition and Christian faith, since both are grounded in God's promises to Israel. But Christ fulfilled these promises and brought an end to the age of Jewish law and temple sacrifices. Christ is the mediator of "a better covenant" (8:6). Christ is,

- Superior to the prophets (1:1-4)
- Superior to the angels (1:5-14)
- Superior to Moses (3:1-6)
- Superior to Joshua (4:1-11)
- Superior to the Jewish Priesthood (4:14-5:10; 7:1-29)

Christ offers a superior sacrifice (10:1-18) and mediates a superior covenant (8:1-13). He intercedes for Christians in a superior heavenly temple (9:1-28). Obviously, the author of Hebrews believes a new time has arrived. Christ inaugurated the new age of fulfillment.

We are told that Jesus appeared "in these last days" (1:2). This is an apocalyptic idea rooted in the Old Testament. It reflects hope in "the day of the Lord." Christians have tasted "the powers of the age to come" (6:5). Christ appeared once at "the end of the age" to offer himself as a sacrifice for sin (9:26). Believers already see "the Day" approaching (10:25). The Old Testament promises and predictions about salvation have been fulfilled in Jesus Christ. This includes the fulfillment of the new covenant,

> For this reason he [Jesus] is the mediator of a new covenant, so that those who are called may receive the promised eternal inheritance, because a death has occurred that redeems them from the transgressions under the first covenant. (9:15)

The old covenant is fulfilled in Jesus. The new covenant has superseded the old covenant in the same way that God's revelation through Christ, the eternal Son and heir of all things, is superior to the fragmentary and diverse revelation of God through the prophets (1:1-3). The Jewish system of sacrifice and atonement has been superseded by the "better" sacrifice of Christ on the cross, "For it is impossible for the blood of bulls and goats to take away sins" (10:4). Those former rituals were merely "a shadow of the good things to come and not the true form of these realities" (10:1). Indeed, "by a single sacrifice he [Christ] has perfected for all time those who are being sanctified" (10:14). In Christ, the time has come "to set things right" (9:10).

To sum up, the new has replaced the old. "And what is obsolete and growing old will soon disappear" (8:13). Christ has replaced the Torah and the temple. Christianity has supplanted Judaism as God's new people of salvation (4:9). Judaism is viewed not as a false religion, but as an incomplete and inferior revelation that has been fulfilled in Jesus Christ. Having served its purpose as a foreshadowing of the salvation to come, Judaism can now disappear or be swallowed up by Christianity. We should keep in mind that Hebrews is a Christian sermon. It was not written to encourage Jewish-Christian dialogue or to promote an ecumenical spirit! It was written to strengthen Christians who were in danger of falling away. This brings us to the topic of pilgrimage.

Pilgrimage and Perseverance

> *Let us run with perseverance the race that is set before us, looking to Jesus.*
>
> *--Hebrews 11:1-2*

The pilgrimage of God's people on earth is one of faith, obedience, suffering, and hope. This world is a transitory place. Nothing lasts forever. All things come to an end. The people of God, according to Hebrews, are strangers and foreigners, passing through time on their way to eternity, seeking a homeland, a better country, and looking forward "to the city that has foundations, whose architect and builder is God" (11:10). Christian eschatology is about the transition from the temporal to the eternal; Hebrews describes this journey as a pilgrimage of faith, obedience, suffering, and hope.

In Christian theology, the community of faithful pilgrims is called "the communion of saints." Salvation is communal. God saves a community, a people. No one walks into the heavenly city alone, and no one walks in without having suffered.

Hebrews emphasizes *the people of God*. Early Christianity had no political clout or economic leverage in society. Christians had no church property or institutionalized bureaucracy. There was no centralized authority except various apostles and evangelists, and some of these were itinerants. How did this loosely bound group of believers manage to survive? They viewed themselves as the people of God, the true descendents of Israel.

According to Hebrews, Christians have joined a long history of faith and obedience. They have spiritual "ancestors" (1:1). They have intimate fellowship with "the assembly of the firstborn who are enrolled in heaven," and with "the spirits of the righteous made perfect" (12:23). Christians are "the descendents of Abraham" because, like Abraham, they live by faith in the promises of God and are heirs "to the righteousness that is in accordance with faith" (2:16; 11:7). Clearly, literal Israel is now in the rearview mirror; spiritual Israel is what matters. This spiritual ancestry includes a great cloud of witnesses and heroes of faith, who believed, obeyed, suffered, and died in hope (11:1-12:1). These faithful ancestors walked the pilgrim path. All endured hardship while clinging to their hope for the coming world. All of them died in faith "without having received the promises" (11:13).

But the history of faith finds its center in Jesus. Pilgrimage is not aimless wandering. Pilgrimage is following the example of Jesus, who is the epitome of faith, obedience, suffering, and hope. Jesus is the real hero of Hebrews. As the eternal Son of God, he became like his brothers and sisters, and was made perfect through suffering, having tasted death for everyone (2:9). He learned obedience through what he suffered (5:8). For the joy set before him, Jesus endured the cross (12:2). Having been raised from the dead and exalted to heaven, he now reigns as Lord "through the power of an indestructible life" (7:16). And he will appear a second time, "not to deal with sin, but to save those who are eagerly waiting for him" (9:28).

Eagerly waiting for the second coming of Christ—here is the eschatological hope that sustains a persecuted pilgrim people. Did these believers think faith would be easy? Did they expect comfort and ease? Hebrews views suffering and persecution as inevitable for those who believe in Christ. If Jesus, the pioneer of our salvation, suffered and died, why should Christians expect any less for themselves? Just as Jesus suffered outside the city of Jerusalem on Golgotha, "let us then go to him outside the camp and bear the abuse he endured. For here we have no lasting city, but we are looking for the city that is to come" (13:13-14).

Perseverance is central to pilgrimage. Christian perseverance is not mere resignation to things as they are. It is triumphant faith and hope in spite of suffering and hard times. The ambiguities of life continue. The age to come is experienced only in fragments, never in perfection. The coming world seems to be taking a long time to arrive. There are many opportunities to quit and to revert to old ways of unbelief. Hebrews is dealing with the troubles that arise for Christians when time drags on.

Two temptations for believers are complacency and apostasy. Complacency is evidenced by creeping indifference. Some Christians were neglecting to meet together for worship and fellowship (10:25). They were forgetting their earlier days when they endured persecution for their faith, even to the point of having their possessions plundered (10:34). Complacency also implies lack of growth in the faith. Hebrews chastises some Christians for getting lazy and for not advancing in knowledge and depth in regard to Christian teaching. They should be eating "solid food" by now. Instead, they are dull and still drinking milk (5:11-14).

Some believers were in danger of apostasy, drifting away from the faith, turning away from God, just as the Israelites had done in the desert for forty years (2:1; 3:12-13). But those who turn back will suffer dire consequences. Having tasted "the powers of the age to come," those who reject this message have no hope for repentance again (6:1-8). The fate of backsliders is not good, for we are talking about God's eschatological community of salvation. Outside this fellowship of salvation there is no salvation. To leave the community is to be lost.

Where would Christians go if they fell away? Perhaps some would go back to their old pagan ways. Others might be drawn toward Judaism, or back to Judaism. This is a common problem for apocalyptic groups. What happens when the end doesn't come? What happens when "the coming world" is delayed? Hebrews was written to encourage Christians to hang on until Christ appears, "For you need endurance, so that when you have done the will of God, you may receive what was promised . . . But we are not among those who shrink back and so are lost, but among those who have faith and so are saved" (10:36, 39). Christians are to endure trials for the sake of discipline (11:7). "Therefore lift your drooping hands and strengthen your weak knees . . ." (12:12). It is not enough to begin as a Christian; one must maintain one's confidence "firm to the end" (3:14).

The good news is that Jesus already walked the path of faith, obedience, suffering, and hope, and he conquered. Hebrews emphasizes solidarity with Christ in his sufferings. Believers had already met with some persecution, but they had not yet shed their blood for the gospel (12:3-4). Moreover, Christ identifies and sympathizes with the weakness of Christians. He is presently available to offer "grace to help in time of need" (4:16). Christians can now enter into the heavenly sanctuary by the blood of Jesus and gain access to God and God's power (10:19-20). The discipline of suffering is unpleasant at the time, but afterwards "it yields the peaceful fruit of righteousness to those who have been trained by it" (11:11).

Hebrews views the church as the pilgrim people of God faithfully following Jesus amidst suffering, complacency, and apostasy, but always looking to the end, to God's eschatological rest.

Eschatological Rest

So then, a sabbath rest still remains for the people of God.

--Hebrews 4:9

Hebrews uses the image of *Sabbath rest* to describe the final aim of history. Just as God rested from all his works on the seventh day, Christians rest from their labors also (through faith) and will experience the true Sabbath rest in God's eschatological kingdom.

Here we see the tension between the "already" and the "not yet" (Ladd 1993:622). Hebrews says, "For we who have believed enter that rest" (4:3). Yet, "Let us therefore make every effort to enter that rest" (4:11). This is a paradox. We've entered God's rest, yet we must strive to enter it. We are already saved, yet we await salvation. We are already experiencing the powers of the coming age, yet we await the fullness of God's kingdom. "Already/Not Yet" is the structure of Christian faith and hope (see Epilogue).

The Israelites failed to enter God's rest (3:12-4:2). Christians are assured, however, that through faith they enter God's Sabbath rest. They are warned to not fall away but to continue to persevere to the end until they experience God's rest in its fullness at the end of the age. Though God's coming judgment is "a consuming fire," Christians can trust that "Jesus Christ is the same yesterday, today, and forever" (12:29; 13:8). This is the source of Christian hope.

Hebrews is not doomsday theology. There is no breathless apocalyptic drama, no Armageddon or Antichrist. Yet Hebrews is entirely eschatological, one of the most eschatological documents in the New Testament. The Book of Revelation, on the other hand, is thoroughly apocalyptic. We will now turn our focus to Revelation.

16

Faithful Witnessing in the Book of Revelation

The Book of Revelation is the most political book in the New Testament. In American history, Revelation has fueled millenarian movements, leading to zealous nationalism and American triumphalism. Revelation has inspired numerous sectarian groups, political anarchy, and violence in the name of God.

One looks for a central theme in Revelation. I have chosen the theme of *faithful witnessing under fire*. Jurgen Moltmann comments, "We don't understand the book of Revelation because we don't understand the martyrs" (Moltmann 2004:91). Revelation is written for Christian martyrs and for those Christians who will soon be martyred. The Greek word for witness is *martus*, from which we get our word "martyr." A martyr is someone who bears faithful witness under fire. Jesus is the supreme witness, the Lamb who was slaughtered and who conquered through his death and resurrection. The faithful martyrs are killed by a hostile, anti-God political power, namely, Rome.

Despite its cryptic symbolism, Revelation is simple in its plot.

It is a Christianized version of the old story of Good vs. Evil. The righteous are oppressed, persecuted, and some of them are killed. But ultimately God triumphs over evil and saves his people. Meanwhile, Jesus stands in the midst of his churches, guiding, rebuking, and comforting. His main message is, "Be faithful until death, and I will give you the crown of life . . . Surely I am coming soon!" (2:10; 22:20). The backdrop of this drama is the persecution of Christians in the latter years of the first century A.D. by the Roman Empire. Rome becomes a universal symbol of "the beast." This beastly, anti-God power is a political force that oppresses the true people of God.

Good News for the Underdog!

Revelation is rooted in a history of suffering. It begins with the suffering of Jesus himself, "The Lamb that was slain." Christians living in the first century were the underdogs. Revelation was probably written in the 90s A.D. At that time Christianity was a small sect in the midst of a pagan empire. Bearing witness to Christ could get a person killed, depending on where one lived.

Apocalyptic literature is resistance literature intended to strengthen God's persecuted people and bring them hope. Revelation is "God to the rescue!" But first, there is suffering. Like Christ himself, Christians must bear witness, even to the point of death. These are the ones Christ loves because they have kept his word and patiently endured their trials (3:9-10). These persecuted Christians are materially poor but spiritually rich (2:9). They hold fast to the name of Jesus and do not deny their faith (2:13). The martyrs are slaughtered for the word of God, and they are in solidarity with Christian martyrs of all ages (6:9-11). They survive "the great ordeal" and have washed their robes "in the blood of the Lamb" (7:14). In the end, God wipes away every tear from their eyes (7:17).

The Christian martyrs refused to worship the beast and its image; they did not cling to life even in the face of death (12:11).

Faithful witnessing under fire and worshiping the true God even if it costs you your life—these themes recur in Revelation.

Underdog spirituality is edgy. Sometimes edginess becomes anger. It is anger rooted in oppression and humiliation, the anger that prays and hopes for a day of vengeance when God will slay the enemy and save his people. Revelation is edgy and angry. The author paints a graphic picture of God's wrath. There are seven seals, seven trumpets, seven last plagues, and those who worship "the beast" will be thrown into "the great wine press of the wrath of God" (14:19). The blood flows. Christ appears with a sickle in his hand (14:14-16). Later he rides in on a white horse to "tread the winepress of the fury of the wrath of God the Almighty" (19:15). This is Christ the warrior king returning to settle an old score. Babylon (Rome) is punished for shedding the blood of saints and prophets (16:6; 18:24). "The great whore" is drunk with the blood of saints and those who remain true to Jesus (17:6). The Devil, the beast, and the false prophet are finally defeated and tossed into a lake of fire with the lost (20:7-15).

Revelation is the voice of the powerless delighting in God's vengeance. Christians were not in a position to raise an army and defeat Rome. All they could do is shoot spit wads at the emperor and hide. Revelation is an apocalyptic spit wad fired at the Roman Empire! It is protest literature. The author wrote a blatant indictment of the Roman Empire, emperor worship, the imperial cult and its priests. He even attacks Judaism. He was on a mission to discredit all religious and political structures of domination.

The First Angel shouts, "Fear God and give him glory, for the hour of his judgment has come; and worship him who made heaven and earth, the sea and the springs of water" (14:7). Proper worship is called for, and no emperor worship. Revelation is about worshiping God the Creator who made heaven and earth (4:11).

Revelation was written by someone named John who was exiled on the island of Patmos in the Aegean Sea, just off the coast of Ephesus. He was persecuted because of the word of God and "the testimony of Jesus" (1:9). John had already suffered as a faithful witness to Jesus Christ. He was writing to other Christians who shared with him "the persecution and the kingdom and the patient endurance" for the sake of Jesus (1:9). Suffering, persecution, and endurance dominate the book of Revelation.

How Extensive was the Persecution?

Christians were not being killed *en masse* in Asia Minor at this time.

It is difficult to document constant collisions between Christians and the Roman Empire in the sub-apostolic period (70-95 A.D.). The reign of Emperor Domitian (81-96 A.D.) was for years viewed as a period of intense persecution of Christians, but this is an overstatement. It is true that later in his career Domitian demanded to be addressed as "our Lord and God." It is also true that the Roman Emperor was viewed as having divine powers and status, and that a powerful imperial cult developed. But regarding ongoing persecutions of Christians, this period of church history is a blank (Frend 1984:148). What we do know is that being a Christian meant living outside the orbit of Roman pagan religion and emperor worship. This could result in clashes with the authorities, but not necessarily. Much depended on the city or region, and who was in charge. Christians who did not participate in emperor worship could be viewed as unpatriotic and subversive (Metzger 1993:16).

Revelation was written at a time when certain Christian communities in Asia Minor were dealing with the issue of emperor worship or accommodation to the surrounding culture. John takes a radical, uncompromising position against Rome and the imperial cult.

Not all Christian communities agreed with John. It would be a mistake to think that all Christians at that time embraced the book of Revelation. Some Christians preached adaptation to culture, not making waves, praying for the emperor and other government authorities, and paying taxes like good citizens (Rom 13:1-7; 1 Tim 2:1-2; 1 Pt 2:13-14). "Fear God and honor the Emperor" seems to be the message, along with living quiet lives and doing good deeds. There is no apocalyptic frenzy in this approach. Can we assume that Christianity at this time was wholly apocalyptic? To impose apocalyptic on the entire Christian movement is a mistake. In fact, one might contend that the doomsday approach was a minority view.

In First Clement, a letter written from Rome to the Christians in Corinth around 96 A.D., we read,

> You, Master, gave them imperial power through your majestic and indescribable might, so that we, recognizing it was you who gave them the glory and honor, might submit to them, and in no way oppose your will. (1 Clement 61:1)

Clement is emphasizing obedience to the political powers. This is a statement about accommodation to culture. Revelation, however, is more closely related to the feisty rhetoric of Jewish apocalyptic. Christians are viewed as a persecuted minority while the Roman Empire is of the Devil and deserves no prayers and no respect. The author of Revelation does not encourage prayers for the emperor!

John's universe is a universe of persecution and martyrdom. Revelation aims at the end of history. History has a purpose and is going somewhere, in spite of hard times and martyrdom. God is guiding history toward fulfillment. Jesus is with his people even now, strengthening them to resist evil and to bear faithful witness to the truth of the gospel. This brings us to the seven churches, my favorite section in Revelation.

The Seven Churches and the Lamb that was Slain

Revelation was written to "the seven churches" (1:4, 11). These churches were real congregations located in the cities of Ephesus, Smyrna, Pergamum, Thyatira, Sardis, Philadelphia, and Laodicea. The risen Jesus had a message for the seven churches (2:1-3:22).

Pheme Perkins (1988:324) points out that the imperial cult was strong in these cities. Ephesus and Smyrna competed for notoriety in honoring the emperor; Pergamum was the regional center of the imperial cult; residents of Thyatira worshiped Apollo incarnate and son of Zeus; and Sardis was in the running for the right to build a temple dedicated to the emperor. Christians had to make a decision: to do their civic duty and participate in emperor worship, or to refuse and suffer the consequences, which might mean economic hardship and perhaps death. This might be the meaning of "the mark of the beast" mentioned in Revelation 13:15-17, which implies that those who do not worship the beast are not allowed to buy or sell.

The letters to the seven churches imply that the persecution of Christians was not universal, nor were all their problems external. Persecution is rarely mentioned in the letters. John envisions impending persecution and possible imprisonment for Christians in Smyrna (2:10), and he refers to a martyr named Antipas (2:13). However, most of John's concerns relate to internal problems: false apostles, heterodox teachings, tensions with Jews, toleration of false doctrines (Balaam, Jezebel, and the Nicolaitans), materialism, sexual immorality, and being "lukewarm" (3:16). Christians had more to fear from inside than outside. The main problem with these churches was libertine doctrines resulting in "a plethora of antinomian schisms" (Frend 1984:137). John warns Christians to repent (2:5; 2:16; 3:19).

Norman Cohn observes, "In fact the Christians in the cities of

Asia—most of them Jewish Christians—led quiet lives and, like other Jews, participated fully in urban society" (Cohn 1993:216). This challenges the view that Christians were being slaughtered at this time. More likely, we see episodic persecutions at the local level. Some Christians had been put to death. Yet all Christians knew their time for martyrdom could come at any moment. They must be ready to follow Jesus even to the point of death.

Therefore, "be faithful until death, and I will give you the crown of life" (2:10); "Strengthen what remains and is on the point of death" (3:2); "Be earnest, therefore, and repent" (3:19). This urgency is rooted in the sense of time running down. John expected his prophecies to be fulfilled soon, within a matter of a few years. He was told to not seal up the prophecy (22:10). He believed an "hour of trial" was near for the whole world (3:10). Jesus is coming soon (1:1; 22:6-7, 12, 20). John ends by saying, "Amen. Come Lord Jesus!" (22:20). In light of the coming judgment, it is imperative for Christians to be *faithful witnesses under fire.*

Jesus is also "the Lamb that was slaughtered." At the center of the book of Revelation is the cross of Christ. He is the premier martyr who leads the way from suffering and death to eternal life. Revelation is Christ-centered apocalyptic.

The exalted Christ is called "the Lamb" twenty-eight times in Revelation. The lamb is an image from Jewish temple worship and the sacrificial cult. Lambs were slaughtered as sacrifices of atonement for the forgiveness of sins. John's theology is steeped in the cross, the sacrificial death of Jesus for the sins of the world. Christians have washed their robes in the blood of the Lamb (7:14). The saints conquer by the blood of the Lamb (12:11).

Animal sacrifices were common in the imperial cult of Rome. In Pergamum, the smoke of sacrifices offered to Zeus ascended twenty-four hours a day non-stop. The smell of animal flesh permeated the air of the city (Metzger 1993:34). Small wonder John said to the Christians in Pergamum, "I know where you are living, where Satan's throne is" (2:13). Christians were called to bear witness to the true sacrifice, the only legitimate sacrifice that could take away sins: the Lamb of God, Jesus Christ.

John's vision of God's throne centers on "a Lamb standing as if it had been slaughtered" (5:6). The Lamb alone is worthy to open the mysterious scroll that unleashes the judgments of God. The reason for his worthiness is that he was slaughtered in order to redeem from humanity God's chosen people, the church (5:9-10).

We might wonder why the image of a sacrificial lamb is transposed into the image of a violent lamb coming to kill his enemies. Here it seems redemptive love turns into redemptive annihilation. Revelation 6:16 describes the wicked shouting to the mountains and rocks, "Fall on us and hide us from the face of the one seated on the throne and from the wrath of the Lamb." This is a jarring image of Jesus. John turns Jesus into a vindictive figure meting out justice by annihilating his enemies. In Revelation 19, Jesus returns on a white horse, carrying a sword and slaying his enemies. But this is the nature of apocalyptic thinking.

Apocalyptic lives in the world of stereotypes. There is no middle ground or compromise. People are either for God or against God. People are either saved or annihilated. The lines are drawn. The worldview is dualistic. Dualism is a literary device that intensifies apocalyptic drama. Thus, Jesus is portrayed as a militant warrior in a battle between God and Satan. This is cosmic warfare at its bloodiest. It is *mythology*. Yet the mythology contains a truth: in the end, God alone is sovereign, and God's people will be delivered. To his credit, John never promotes violence or encourages Christians to take up arms in order to hasten the end.

Revelation is not a strategy for social reform. John believed in the imminent end of all things. There was no time to reform society. The end was near. The world was too corrupt to save. The only hope was the return of Christ.

This has led to an interesting observation by Rudolf Bultmann, "The Christianity of Revelation is a weakly Christianized Judaism . . . Hence the present is understood in a way not basically different from the understanding of it in Jewish apocalypses, namely, as a time of temporariness, of waiting" (Bultmann 1955, 2:175). Waiting for salvation from on high—this is what God's people do while the world is coming unglued. No zealous retaliation, no revolutionary violence, no political involvement. For John, Christians take a stand, bear witness to the truth nonviolently, and wait for the coming of Christ. They "endure" (1:9; 2:2-3, 19; 3:10; 13:10; 14:12).

How shall we apply Revelation to our times?

Revelation Today?

There always seems to be someone shouting, "Revelation was written for our times! It's all coming true!" Such persons view current events as the exact fulfillment of Bible prophecy.

I believe Revelation is applicable to Christians in every age and is always relevant. It is Christian literature and is part of the New Testament. Christians should read it prayerfully. Pastors should preach it.

The themes in Revelation repeat themselves again and again, including the theme *faithful witnessing under fire.* Whenever domination systems dehumanize people and threaten the truth of the gospel, Revelation is relevant. Whenever Christians are being persecuted, as they are in places in the Middle East and Africa today, Revelation is relevant. Whenever the memory of the martyrs is held sacred and leads to resisting injustice, the message of Revelation is relevant: *Do not forget the martyrs, resist oppression, and seek justice.* This should be nonviolent action, not terrorism.

The book of Revelation never gets old. It is not a play-by-play script of last day events. Rather, Revelation is about faithful witnessing under fire and worshiping the true God, even if it costs you your life. Each generation of Christians must search its soul and determine what faithfulness to Jesus Christ really means. Remember the martyrs!

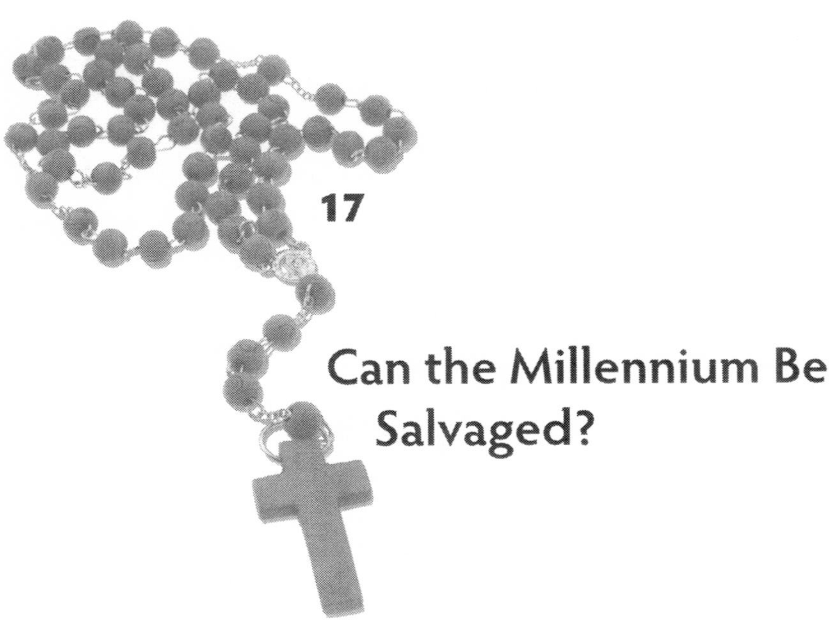

17 Can the Millennium Be Salvaged?

The millennium, in Christian theology, refers to the one-thousand years reign of Christ at the end of time. It is a vision of paradise on earth. The millennium is the ideal time when lions lie down with lambs, and fig trees produce bumper crops year around. There are no wars. It is the time of universal peace with Jesus in charge.

The millennium is the cry of the human heart for a happy ending. Don't we all want a happy ending? At some deep level of our psyche each of us is a millennialist. But frankly, more nonsense has been written about the millennium than any other eschatological symbol. Political revolutionaries have exploited the millennium in an attempt to establish a so-called "perfect society." American theologians, such as Jonathan Edwards in the eighteenth century, viewed America as God's New Israel that would usher in the millennial kingdom. Dispensationalists believe the millennium is a literal Jewish kingdom centered in Jerusalem, with a literal temple, and ruled by "King Jesus."

As we shall see, there is no consensus on the millennium in Christian theology, and there never has been. The *only* explicit reference to the millennium in the New Testament is three verses! Revelation 20:4-6 states,

> Then I saw thrones, and those seated on them were given authority to judge. I also saw the souls of those who had been beheaded for their testimony to Jesus and for the word of God. They had not worshiped the beast or its image and had not received its mark on their foreheads or their hands. They came to life and reigned with Christ a thousand years. (The rest of the dead did not come to life until the thousand years were ended.) This is the first resurrection. Blessed and holy are those who share in the first resurrection. Over these the second death has no power, but they will be priests of God and of Christ, and they will reign with him a thousand years.

We will soon analyze these verses in detail. For now, we note that this passage is about Christian martyrs reigning with Christ. It is not about political revolution, nationalistic patriotism, or a Jewish kingdom in Jerusalem.

Some Christians believe Christ will return to earth prior to the millennium and set up his millennial kingdom. This is called *premillennialism.* Other Christians believe Christ will return after the millennium, that is, after a long period of universal peace. This is called *postmillennialism.*

A third group believes there is no literal millennium; the millennium is a symbol for the final reign of the martyrs and saints. This is called *amillennialism.* This is my position. I do not believe in a literal millennium. I view the millennium as an eschatological symbol. The millennium is a metaphor for the vindication of the martyrs at the end of time. These are the faithful who have laid down their lives for the sake of Christ. They sing a "new song" that no one else can sing. They are a special group, the "first fruits" of the redeemed (14:3-4).

An Ancillary Symbol of Hope

The millennium is a symbol of hope, yet it is not the central symbol of Christianity. Belief in the millennium is not essential to Christian faith. Differing viewpoints regarding the millennium are a minor issue, except for die-hard literalists. Christian faith is not faith in the millennium.

It is doubtful that Jesus taught the millennium. Paul makes no explicit reference to it. Nor can one argue a convincing case for the millennium from the Old Testament, although I believe it has its roots in the idea of a temporal messianic age prior to the final kingdom of God. Revelation presents a Christianized reinterpretation of an earthly messianic age for a thousand years before the coming of God's transcendent kingdom. This is a Jewish idea that has been reworked from the perspective of Christian eschatology.

There is no consensus on the millennium in Christianity. In the second century, diverse Christian writers and preachers differed in their views about the millennium. Whether it was Papias, Justin Martyr, Irenaeus, or Augustine—different thinkers had different ideas on this topic. Origen condemned millennial beliefs and a literal approach to apocalyptic. The Eastern Orthodox Church has tended to reject millennialism. Martin Luther and John Calvin had no use for millennial groups but viewed them as anarchists. Jaroslav Pelikan comments,

> It would seem that very early in the post-apostolic era millenarianism was regarded as a mark neither of orthodoxy nor of heresy, but as one permissible opinion among others within a range of permissible opinions. (Pelikan 1971:125)

A key word here is "opinion." Millennial beliefs are opinions, not essential doctrines. Belief in the millennium is an option for Christians. The optional character of millennial belief is acknowledged even by evangelical scholars. For example, Millard J. Erickson (1977) and Stanley J. Grenz (1992) use the word "options" in the titles of their books on the millennium. Such scholars acknowledge the difficulties of interpreting the millennium. There is enough obscurity to necessitate toleration of variant views. Grenz, by the way, offers an impressive overview of millennial positions through the centuries of church history, as does Thomas C. Oden (1992:421-430).

Given the diversity of opinion on the millennium, can it be salvaged as an eschatological symbol? How important is the millennium to Christian faith? It certainly is not an essential doctrine. Nevertheless, this chapter is an attempt to salvage the millennium as an ancillary symbol of Christian hope.

The Millennium and the Martyrs

As we saw in the previous chapter, Revelation is martyr theology. It was written in the late first century in the context of persecution. Some Christians were being slain for their testimony to Jesus and for the word of God. It was not universal persecution, but probably localized. Christians refused to participate in emperor worship and some were martyred. Revelation is a tribute to those who did not worship "the beast."

Revelation 19 and 20 describe a cosmic melodrama. To paraphrase, the beast and the false prophet are thrown into the lake of fire at the coming of Christ, and the wicked are destroyed (19:20-21). Christ is a warrior-messiah. Some Jewish apocalyptic writers viewed the Messiah as a warrior who would set up his kingdom in Jerusalem for a certain period of time before "the end" (Rist 1962:381). Here is the first hint of a millennial kingdom on earth ruled by the Messiah. Satan is bound for a thousand years but not annihilated (20:1-3). Jesus has returned and killed everyone who worshipped the beast and his image. The beast and the false prophet are also killed. Satan is imprisoned. *Who's left on planet earth?* We can only assume that everyone is dead except . . .

Suddenly, thrones are set up and the martyrs are raised from the dead and rule with Christ for a thousand years. *Where?* The text does not say. Is it in heaven? Is it on earth? Who else is alive during this reign? In other words, the millennium as an image of an earthly utopia (or a Jewish kingdom) cannot be justified from the text. It is a bogus dream.

When the thousand years are over, Satan is set loose on the world in order to deceive the nations. *The nations?* Who are these nations? Isn't everyone dead? Satan makes a final assault on "the camp of the saints." *Where is this camp?* Fire comes down from heaven and destroys them all. Then oddly enough, they are all resurrected again to face the final judgment and be killed again (20:7-15). This is the twisted and tortuous tale of the millennial kingdom as described in Revelation 20.

The millennium is apocalyptic mythology, not a literal event. There is nothing historical about this passage of scripture. Rather, it paints a mythological picture of an interim and earthly messianic kingdom ruled by Christ and the martyrs. Martyr theology is at work here. Will the martyrs be vindicated? The millennium is the answer: Yes! No one who dies for the word of God dies in vain. They will be raised incorruptible and will reign with Christ during a one-thousand years messianic age prior to the age to come. This is a Christianized version of Jewish messianic hope for an earthly messianic kingdom. The millennium is Christianized Jewish apocalyptic.

The fact is Revelation says very little about the millennium. Bauckham & Hart write,

> The millennium in fact fulfills one very specific function within the visionary narrative of Revelation. It portrays the vindication of the martyrs which Christ's victory over the earthly powers of evil at his parousia must entail . . . The image of the millennial reign, as employed here, portrays

the vindication of the martyrs at the parousia. (Bauckham & Hart 1999:134-35)

Bauckham & Hart suggest that a literal reading of the millennium makes it incomprehensible and produces dubious ideas of Christian utopianism. For example, is Revelation 20:4-6 describing the gradual advance of the kingdom of God within society until we achieve a just social order here on earth? Are these verses describing a literal earthly kingdom in a literal Jerusalem for literal Jews who have been converted to Christ and who worship at a literal temple with literal priests? In short, is Revelation 20:4-6 describing anything that will actually occur within history? My answer is no.

In summary, the millennium is a symbol of the reign of the martyrs with Christ. It highlights those who did not worship the "beast" and who died for their faith. The millennium is a Christian reworking of the Jewish hope for an earthly messianic age; it is not a literal period of time. It is a *temporal* vision of a *transcendent* hope. The martyrs sing a "new song" that no one else can sing; they will always be a special group, the "first fruits" of the redeemed (14:3-4).

A Final Note on Salvaging Symbols

The symbolic interpretation of the millennium is often criticized for not taking seriously the truth of a literal millennium on earth. I would argue that the symbolic interpretation is the best interpretation if one is faithful to the context of Revelation and the author's intention. Symbols can be salvaged only as we stick to the context of the text. Revelation is apocalyptic mythology, not a program of literal last day events described sequentially.

Moreover, neither premillennialism nor postmillennialism remains true to Revelation 20:4-6. These views are dubious embellishments of the text. Each of them forces the text to say something that it does not say. Each of these "options" is no option at all if one stays true to the original passage of scripture.

Finally, symbols can be salvaged only if they are directly related to the gospel of Jesus Christ. The millennium is an eschatological symbol of hope when it is viewed in its original and limited meaning: *the martyrs will be vindicated at the end of time, for God will have the last word.* These are ones who lived cruciform lives and who died a cruciform death for the crucified Christ, who is still being crucified today in his persecuted people.

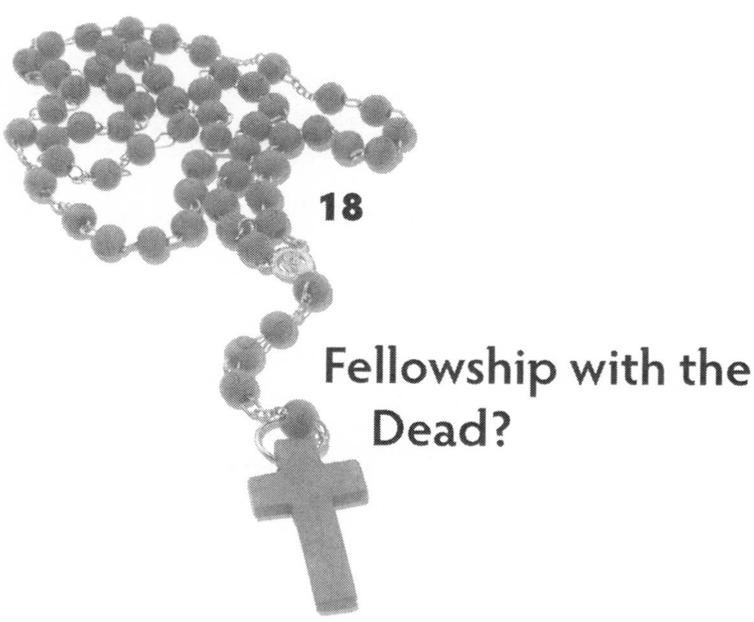

18

Fellowship with the Dead?

Death is of course the limit of our lives, but it is not the limit of God's relationship to us.

--Jurgen Moltmann

I was raised in a church that believed the dead are really dead. We didn't pray for the dead. We never lit candles in memory of the dead. We never talked about "the communion of saints." The dead were asleep and that was that.

The dead were either saved or lost. The saved didn't go to heaven right away; they stayed in the grave, unconscious, until the last day when Jesus would resurrect them. The lost were also locked into their fate, lying in the grave awaiting the final judgment. In other words, the dead—both the saved and the lost—were underground and didn't know anything.

There certainly was no fellowship between the living and dead. The dead are not present with us. This was my childhood introduction to the state of the dead. Traditionally, this is called "soul sleep." Many Christians, including Martin Luther, believed this. The fancy name is *psychopannychism.* Others who held this view were

William Tyndale, John Milton, and Isaac Newton. Modern groups that teach soul sleep include Jehovah's Witnesses and Seventh-day Adventists.

Is there fellowship with the dead? Where are the dead? Is there a lasting community with the dead? Are the dead sleeping or in purgatory or in hell or in heaven with Jesus? Do the dead remember us? How should we remember them? Should we pray on behalf of the dead?

Two questions frame this discussion,

- Does God's relationship of love and grace extend beyond the grave and embrace the dead?
- Is Christ the Lord of the dead as well as the living?

I have concluded that the idea of fellowship with the dead must begin and end with God's grace and the kingdom of God as the ultimate aim of human destiny. My views are informed by an understanding of the church as "the communion of saints." It was ecclesiology that led to my rejection of soul sleep. My "theology of the dead" is derived from my theology of the church. *Ecclesiology shapes thanatology*. Yet I acknowledge the fact of ambiguity in regard to the state of the dead.

A Reminder about Ambiguity

No human being is unambiguously on one side or the other of divine judgment.

--Paul Tillich

There is no official consensus about "the intermediate state." There is enough mystery here to make one pause and consider the fact of ambiguity. In regard to the dead we can only speculate. Thomas C. Oden describes what most Christians believe about the intermediate state,

> The souls of the just are conscious of their joy in the presence of Christ after death and before resurrection. The souls of the unjust are conscious of their absence from the glory of the Lord after death and before resurrection. Both enter immediately after death into an intermediate state of awaiting final judgment. (Oden 1992:391)

According to Oden, *most* Christians do not believe in soul sleep; they believe the dead are conscious of being either included in Christ or excluded from Christ. Included or excluded? Everlastingly saved or everlastingly lost? None of this can be proven. We are confronted with ambiguity.

Ambiguity is the awareness of our partial knowledge. Paul said it best in his hymn to love, "For we know only in part, and we prophesy only in part; but when the complete comes, the partial will come to an end" (1 Cor 13:9-10). What matters is not exhaustive knowledge regarding divine mysteries, but faith, hope, and love. These three Christian virtues cover a multitude of questions.

Yet Christians live in anticipation of fullness. There is something incomplete about this world and about our knowledge. We wait for fullness and hope for completion. We lean into God's coming future. We have tasted a part of it through baptism, the Eucharist, and life in the Spirit. But God's future has not come in its fullness. This is the eschatological assumption of our views regarding the dead.

Because we have not yet experienced fullness, ambiguity is a trait of what it means to be human. John tells us, "Beloved, we are God's children now; what we will be has not been revealed. What we do know is this: when he is revealed, we will be like him, for we will see him as he is" (1 Jn 3:2). As children of God, we do have some assurance. However, much has not been revealed at this time. Ambiguity remains. In the end, we will be like Christ, united with him for eternity in a fellowship of love. This hope remains, in spite of ambiguity regarding "the intermediate state."

In the sixteenth century, John Calvin addressed this issue in his *Institutes of the Christian Religion*. He wrote,

> Now it is neither lawful nor expedient to inquire too curiously concerning our souls' intermediate state. Many torment themselves overmuch with disputing as to what place the souls occupy and whether or not they already enjoy heavenly glory. Yet it is foolish and rash to inquire concerning unknown matters more deeply than God permits us to know. (McNeil 1960, 2:997)

Calvin was dogmatic on many points, but in regard to the state of the dead he wisely resisted pontificating.

The Bible itself is ambiguous on the state of the dead. In regard to what happens when we die, the Bible speaks in a number of contradictory voices. For every text supporting soul sleep, we can find other texts implying that the dead in Christ are with Christ now, experiencing blessed peace.

Human nature is ambiguous as well. Christian theology teaches that we are sinners and saints at the same time. No one is perfect, and the greatest saints admit this. In the heart of every saint is a sinner, and in the heart of every sinner is a saint. Even the most unfulfilled life has positive elements in it, and these elements are signs of grace. The image of God persists to some degree in even the most distorted person. This is why absolute judgments over the dead are impossible. We might use language such as "saved and lost," but as finite creatures can we determine the ultimate destiny of a person? Not even Paul judged himself but cast himself on the gracious judgment of Christ at the end of time (1 Cor 4:3-6). We don't know who is saved or lost, and we would be wise to withhold judgment about anyone's ultimate destiny.

What I do know is that the church throughout the centuries has believed in and taught "the communion of saints." This implies solidarity with the living and the dead.

Solidarity with the Living and the Dead

Those who gather to worship God in the name of Jesus are never alone.

--*Robert Ellsberg*

Over the years ministry to the sick and the dying has shaped my views of fellowship with the dead. Serving the dying and their families, conducting funerals and leading prayers and hymns, standing by the graveside and offering words of consolation, leading grief groups and doing bereavement follow-up, and the deaths of friends and family members—these experiences have deepened my understanding of "the communion of saints."

The Apostles' Creed says, "I believe in the communion of saints." What is meant by this?

Saints are not sinless, semi-divine beings. In the New Testament, saints are fallible, sinful people who have responded to the gospel and been baptized into the church. The saints are those who have been called by God in Jesus Christ and who try to live according to the Spirit. The communion of saints is the church. When Christians recite the Creed they are saying, "I believe in the church as the fellowship of Jesus. This fellowship includes the living and the dead."

Belief in the communion of saints means affirming our solidarity with the dead, with former generations of Christians who have gone before us.

G. K. Chesterton said that tradition is "the democracy of the dead." Whenever we honor a tradition, we are giving the dead a vote and allowing the dead have a say in how we do things. In the same way, remembering the dead is acknowledging their abiding presence among us. To pray on behalf of the dead is to make them present to us, mentally and spiritually.

It was common for Christians in the first few centuries to gather at the graveside of their dead. It was their way of acknowledging the dead and their witness to Christ. This was the beginning of "the cult of saints." This movement came from below, not from the hierarchy. Regular Christians living their day-to-day lives wanted and needed to honor the dead, especially the martyrs. For those early Christians, solidarity with the dead meant solidarity with the Christian martyrs. The martyrs lived on in the sacred memory and the prayers of the church.

Thus, the communion of saints became a statement about the *extensiveness* of the church—past, present, and future. We are surrounded by a great company of witnesses, and with this company we persevere, keeping our eyes on Jesus (Heb 12:1-2). It's about solidarity and continuity.

At every baptism, at every Eucharist, at every funeral, and in the intercessions and songs, the church affirms its link to the past and its future hope. This is why a Christian view of death is not only about individual eschatology or personal salvation. A Christian theology of death begins and ends with God's purposes in history: the consummation of all things in Jesus Christ. This brings us to the final two parts of this essay: the lordship of Christ over the dead, and God's ongoing relationship with the dead.

Descent into Hell?

> *He was crucified, died, and was buried; he descended into hell.*
>
> --*The Apostles' Creed*

The most curious statement in the Apostles' Creed is the old phrase, "He descended into hell." It is a "wildly mythological" concept (Macquarrie 1990:139). What does it mean to say that Christ descended into hell?

When translating a religious symbol we must inquire about the motive behind the symbol. What is the symbol driving at? We can then discern the core theological meaning of the symbol for faith.

Christ's descent into hell is a symbolic idea conveying a truth about Christ and the dead.

Ancient cosmology envisioned a three-tiered universe: heaven-earth-under the earth. God lived in heaven, humans lived on earth, and the dead existed in a dark cavern under the earth. In the Old Testament this "underworld" is called *sheol*: the realm of the dead, both the just and the unjust. The New Testament word for *sheol* is *hades*. Hades is not hell. It is not a place of eternal torment and punishment. Rather, it is a place of shadows and silence, a place of forgetfulness and separation from the vision of God (Ps 6:5; 88:12; Job 10:21-22; Eccl 9:10). The impression is that Hades (or *sheol*) is a gigantic warehouse where the dead are stored temporarily until their fate is decided. It isn't hell and it isn't heaven; it is the netherworld. This, according to the Creed, is where Christ went during the interval between his death and resurrection. What did he do there? Whatever it was, it was wildly mythological!

We might wonder about the people who died prior to Christ. What about all the folks in Hades? Will they be saved, too? What about those who never heard the gospel? What about the people of Noah's day, the patriarchs, the prophets, infants, etc. Are they lost or saved? Is there still hope for them? To put it theologically: *Do the benefits of Christ's redemption extend backward as well as forward?* Christ's descent into Hades answers this question. The salvation of Christ points forward but also backward. I think this is the meaning of two obscure passages in the New Testament,

> He was put to death in the flesh, but made alive in the spirit, in which he also went and made a proclamation to the spirits in prison, who in former times did not obey, when God waited patiently in the days of Noah, during the building of the ark, in which a few, that is, eight persons were saved through water. (1 Pt 3:18-20)
>
> For this is the reason the gospel was proclaimed even to the dead, so that, though they had been judged in the flesh

as everyone is judged, they might live in the spirit as God does. (1 Pt 4:6)

These verses point to a concern for people prior to Christ, before Jesus died on the cross for their sins. The benefits of Christ's atonement mysteriously apply to them as well. The idea of Christ proclaiming salvation in *sheol* is a mythological image of God's commitment to the dead. Christ went to Hades "in spirit" to liberate the dead. The phrase "He descended to the dead" expresses solidarity and lordship, and the possibility of salvation for pre-Christian persons (Kung 1993:99). This idea comes very close to universalism by implying (shockingly) that the dead, too, can arrive at faith.

The dead are not forgotten by Christ. This is the message of the Creed. Christ is the Lord of both the living and the dead: "Do not be afraid; I am the first and the last, and the living one. I was dead, and see, I am alive forever and ever; and I have the keys of Death and Hades" (Rev 1:17-18). Paul envisions the future time when every being in heaven and earth and *under the earth* will confess that Jesus is Lord (Phil 2:9-11).

We might view the dead at this time to be with Christ and in Christ, awaiting the resurrection. They are not yet totally saved, but they are not eternally lost. They are part of Christ's fellowship, for Christ has claimed the dead as his own. Yet like all of us, they await the final appearance of God's kingdom in glory.

This brings us to God's ongoing relationship with the dead.

God Knows Your Name

Do not fear, for I have redeemed you; I have called you by name, you are mine.

--Isaiah 43:1

There are no anonymous deaths in the heart and mind of God. There are no unidentified bodies. No corpses waiting to be claimed. No impersonal morgues. We have a name. God knows our name. God knows my life, and God will know my death. God will continue to know and love me beyond death into the New Creation. This is true of all of us.

This is the meaning of Isaiah 43:1, "Do not fear, for I have redeemed you; I have called you by name." We do not lose our identities at death. God knows our name. Paul wrote, "Your life is hidden with Christ in God" (Col 3:3). Even now our true identities live in the heart of God and are "hidden," kept safe forever until the final coming of God's kingdom.

Annihilation? As someone who has conducted many funerals, I can attest that there is no "good news" in the concept of annihilation. There is no gospel in the belief that everyone who dies is annihilated and ceases to exist from that point on. God has created us in his image, and each person is a unique creation of God. God's Spirit lives in our spirit and testifies to us that we are children of God (Rom 8:15-16). If death meant total annihilation of the person, then God would be revoking his relationship to human beings created in the image of God—*Imago dei.* But I believe that God holds us in death just as God holds us in life. Death does not end our relationship with God because death does not end God's relationship with us.

In the preface to the Catholic Requiem Mass, it says, "life changes, but it is not taken away." This is a good approach to fellowship with the dead. The dead have been changed, yet they still exist. God's relationship to us is stronger than death.

Conclusion

> *Grant them your peace; let light perpetual shine upon them.*
>
> --*Prayer for the dead*

If we are indifferent toward the dead, we will become indifferent toward the living. If we ignore the martyrs, we will eventually ignore violence, injustice, and oppression. If we live only for the present, we will never learn from the past nor understand God's coming future. There is a certain measure of arrogance and narcissism in forgetting the dead.

Furthermore, what about our prayers? If our prayers do not acknowledge the dead, doesn't our spirituality become narrow? Are we not robbed of fellowship with the saints, robbed of the spiritual power that comes from the Spirit working through "the spirits of the righteous made perfect" (Heb 12:23). Christian community is broad and includes both the dead and the living. Our prayers should reflect this bond.

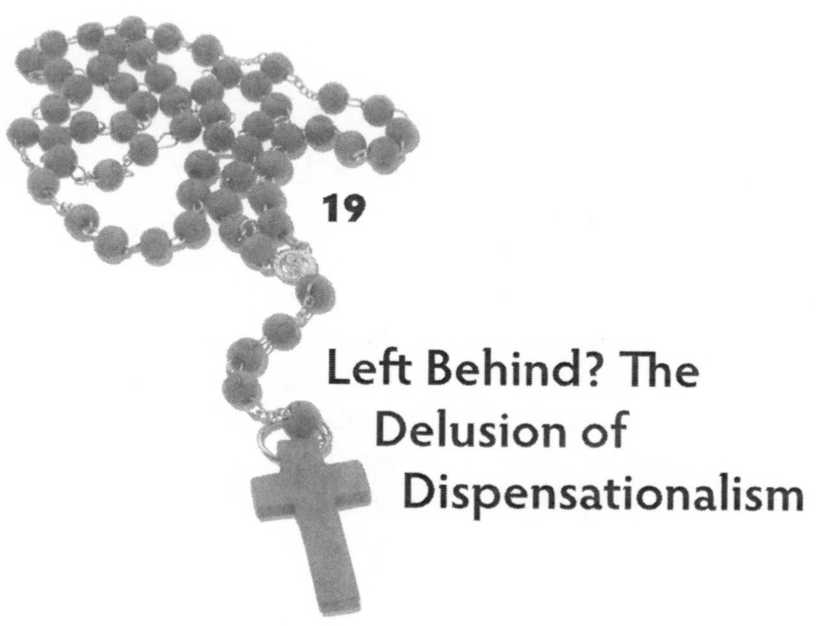

19 Left Behind? The Delusion of Dispensationalism

Are you going to be left behind when Jesus raptures the church to heaven? Here are a few more questions:

- Does the Holy Land belong exclusively to Israel?
- Does God have a separate plan for Israel and another plan for the church?
- Is the Battle of Armageddon a literal battle?
- Is the Millennial Kingdom a Jewish kingdom centered in Jerusalem?

The above beliefs are part of a theological package called *dispensationalism.* Technically, it is *dispensational premillennialism.* Premillennial is the belief that Christ will return before the millennium, before the 1000-years of peace described in Revelation 20. In this essay, I offer an overview and critique of normative dispensationalism. I will address,

- The inerrancy of the Bible
- Consistent literalism

- Futurist premillennialism
- Dispensations
- The distinction between Israel and the church
- The pretribulation Rapture

Where is dispensationalism on the Christian map? Generally speaking, dispensationalism is the eschatology of Christian fundamentalism. Most fundamentalists embrace dispensationalist ideas. According to Timothy P. Weber, dispensationalism is currently believed by about one-third of American evangelicals (Moyers 2007). Evangelicals, on the whole, reject dispensationalism. Liberal churches view dispensationalism as a freak theological mutation.

The dispensationalist Bible is the *Scofield Reference Bible*, originally produced by Cyrus I. Scofield and first published in 1909. There is also the *Ryrie Study Bible*, an annotated version by Charles C. Ryrie. Dispensationalism has been popularized by writers and preachers, such as Pat Robertson, John Hagee, Hal Lindsey, Tim LaHaye, and Grant R. Jeffrey.

In dispensationalism we encounter a special vocabulary: Rapture, pre-Trib, mid-Trib, post-Trib, Antichrist, the Beast, the "false prophet," Gog and Magog, Armageddon, the Blessed Hope, the Glorious Appearing, and the Millennial Kingdom. These concepts are precisely used. For example, the Blessed Hope refers to the Rapture, and the Glorious Appearing refers to the second coming of Christ. Normative dispensationalism is pre-Trib—first the Rapture occurs, then the Tribulation.

But what are we talking about?

Dispensationalism is hermeneutics. It is a method of interpreting Bible prophecy in a literal manner that results in an exotic understanding of Israel and the church. Some people think that dispensationalism is primarily about last-day events, but it is really about ecclesiology: *the doctrine of the church and its relation to Israel.* The Rapture is not the center of dispensationalism. Israel is the center.

In fact, "without Israel, the whole plan falls apart" (Weber 1998:41). Israel always means literal Israel, never spiritual Israel.

Dispenationalism presupposes two covenants and two separate plans of salvation. One plan is for Christians, the other plan is for Jews. God saves Christians on one track and Jews on another track; both plans reach fulfillment in their own time. Keep in mind two covenants, two separate plans, and the literal fulfillment of prophecies regarding Israel. This is why dispensationalists are obsessed with Israel. Politically, they are pro-Israel and believe that Israel will play a central role in last day events before the end of time. Dispensationalists believe that the establishment of Israel as a nation in 1948 was the fulfillment of Bible prophecy.

How and when did these views evolve? In the nineteenth century, and through a man named John Nelson Darby. Dispensationalism is Darbyism, but it has evolved over the years.

An Evolving Tradition

Dispensationalism is an evolving subtradition of American evangelicalism (Blaising & Bock 1992). It started with John Nelson Darby (1800-1882). In the nineteenth century, Darby came to the United States from England. He had been a deacon in the Church of England (in Ireland) and was preparing to be ordained a priest when he became disillusioned with institutional religion. Darby shifted gears and joined the Plymouth Brethren. He had a sharp intellect, effective speaking and writing skills, and a vast knowledge of the Bible. Darby was a sectarian. Fundamentalist in his outlook, he brought dispensationalism to America.

Eventually Dwight L. Moody (1837-1899) embraced dispensationalism and popularized it through the Moody Bible Institute of Chicago. But Cyrus I. Scofield (1843-1921) was the most famous American promoter of dispensationalism. A former lawyer and Episcopalian, Schofield underwent a conversion experience in his 30's and was won over to the new theology. In 1909 he published the *Scofield Reference Bible.* In a few years it sold two million copies and remains the classic text of dispensational thought. Dispensationalism took on institutional form in 1924 when Evangelical Theological College was founded by Lewis S. Chafer. It was later renamed Dallas Theology Seminary and has become a major center for training dispensationalist clergy. Through high profile fundamentalist preachers and television personalities, dispensationalism has attained a status that Darby and Scofield could never have imagined.

There are varieties of dispensationalism. Dispensationalists are on a journey of self-definition. Like all theological systems, there are phases of development,

(1) **Original Dispensationalism**—*Plymouth Brethren, John Nelson Darby.*

(2) **Confessional Dispensationalism**—*Cyrus I. Scofield, Lewis S. Chafer.*

(3) **Classical Dispensationalism**—*Charles C. Ryrie, John F. Walvoord, J. Dwight Pentecost.*

(4) **Popular Dispensationalism**—*Hal Lindsey, Tim LaHaye, Pat Robertson, John Hagee, Grant R. Jeffrey.*

(5) **Progressive Dispensationalism**—*Craig A. Blaising, Darrell L. Bock.*

Each generation of dispensational theologians has put its own spin on things while attempting to preserve continuity with its roots. Again, we will be looking at six features of normative dispensationalism. A counterpoint is offered to each claim.

Six Main Features

1. **Inerrancy** of the Bible. Inerrancy can be defined as, *"The Scriptures of the Old and New Testaments are without error or misstatement in their moral and spiritual teaching and record of historical facts. They are without error or defect of any kind"* (Talbot Theological Seminary website). The idea is that scripture is inspired by God and is error-free.

Inerrancy is more central to dispensationalism than biblical literalism. Inerrancy leads logically to literalism, for the two are related (Barr 1978). How so? Dispensationalists believe the Bible contains error-free information not only regarding morals but about the future. This means error-free information about all the events leading up to the end of time. Bible prophecies are seen as blueprints. Because the Bible is God's error-free Word, it must be accurate in every detail, including details about the end-times. Therefore, it must be literally interpreted.

Counterpoint. Inspiration does not imply inerrancy. A person can believe in the inspiration of scripture without believing in inerrancy. Inspiration and inerrancy are two different things. Dispensationalists live in "the inerrancy loop"—because the Bible is inspired it is inerrant, and the inerrancy of the Bible proves that it is inspired. There is no escaping this loop other than redefining the meaning of inspiration.

The inspiration of the Bible does not mean that the Bible is error-free. It means the Bible is *a reliable guide in matters pertaining to salvation*. Not only this, apocalyptic literature is symbolic and metaphorical by nature. To use apocalyptic as a literal guide for future predictions has resulted in many embarrassing and destructive farces. We can affirm that the Bible is the word of God in the words of humans. Despite contradictions, discrepancies and historical errors, the scriptures are inspired but not inerrant. An error-free Bible is not necessary to Christian faith.

2. Consistent literalism. A literal interpretation of the Bible is the basis of dispensationalism. Charles C. Ryrie says, "Dispensationalism is the only system that practices the principle of literal interpretation consistently" (Ryrie 2007:171). The dispensational system stands or falls on what is termed "consistent literalism."

It is asserted that many, if not most, of the Old Testament prophecies regarding Israel will be literally fulfilled. This includes God's promise of land to Abraham. Numerous Jewish fundamentalists in Israel are willing to construct illegal settlements or even kill Palestinians to fulfill this promise. The biblical promise of land, if taken literally, extends from Egypt to the Euphrates River (modern-day Iraq).

Another example relates to the millennium. Dispensationalists believe that the millennium described in Revelation 20 will be a literal Jewish kingdom here on earth with Jerusalem as its capital. This Jewish kingdom will include daily blood sacrifices in the temple, "and a powerful King Jesus reigning from Jerusalem and exercising Jewish hegemony over the rest of the world" (Weber 1983:23).

A literal interpretation of the Bible, according to John F. Walvoord, means "normal" or "ordinary." Walvoord writes,

> In the literal method, the words of Scripture are understood as indicated by the context in their ordinary, normal, customary usage. . . . The concept of the literal method is that while occasionally allegory and figurative language are used in Scripture, these instances are plainly indicated and can be interpreted alongside other portions which are clearly literal. (Walvoord 1993:10)

Counterpoint. No one doubts that portions of the Bible should be taken literally while other portions are symbolic or allegorical. The issue is what does "normal" mean in relation to cryptic Bible prophecies pregnant with symbolism and numerology? What is the normal reading of apocalyptic literature? What is the ordinary reading of texts dealing with Israel's restoration at the end of time? How does one interpret typology, symbolism, or the Old Testament in light of the New Testament?

Christians of good faith can disagree about what the Bible says regarding the cryptic sections of scripture. Moreover, a rigid literalism can actually pervert the meaning of scripture. We see, for instance, that the New Testament reinterprets Israel in light of Jesus Christ. The first few generations of Christians struggled with this issue, but in the end they redefined Israel in spiritual terms. Paul did not interpret the Old Testament prophecies about Israel in a literal manner but spiritualized them, even saying "not all Israelites truly belong to Israel" (Rom 9:6). For Paul, "real circumcision is a matter of the heart—it is spiritual and not literal" (Rom 2:29). Thus the church was viewed as the spiritual fulfillment of ancient Israel. The church is the new people of God, according to the New Testament.

3. **Futurist premillenialism.** Bible prophecy is all about the future, according to dispensational theology. Walvoord says, "Prophecy is the doctrine of Scripture dealing with predictions of events that will occur in the future" (Walvoord 1993:6). Dispensationalists do not believe that any prophecies are being fulfilled at this time. The prophetic time clock has stopped for the time being, since this is "the time of the Gentiles" when non-Jews hear the gospel and are saved. It is called "the Church Age." All prophecies regarding literal Israel are on hold. God is busy getting the church ready for the Rapture. After the Rapture, prophecies will kick in again, especially those concerning Israel. This is called "futurist premillennialism."

Counterpoint. The key issue here is the nature of Bible prophecy. Predictive prophecy exists in the Bible, but it is not the norm. Moreover, many "predictions" are after the fact (see Chapter Three). To define prophecy as prediction narrows the scope. In the Bible, prophecy means to speak the word of God. This is prophetic eschatology and is the dominant form of prophecy in the Bible. The prophetic message calls for social justice that reflects God's righteousness. Prophets like Amos, Hosea, Isaiah, and Jeremiah preached ethics. Yet dispensationalists focus on the future fulfillment of unfulfilled prophecies. History becomes the predestined unfolding of ancient prophecies literally applied to the future and primarily dealing with Israel. The dispensational view of history is deterministic, and its view of prophecy is one-sided.

4. **Dispensations.** Dispensationalists divide salvation history into seven parts called "dispensations." Ryrie acknowledges that this sevenfold scheme "is neither inspired or nonnegotiable" (Ryrie 2007:58). Nonetheless, classical dispensationalism has settled on the number seven. Each dispensation is marked by a test and is "a distinctive stage in the progress of revelation . . . not for the purpose of enlightening God but for the purpose of bringing out what is in people, whether faith or failure" (Ryrie 2007:40-41).

Following Darby, Scofield listed the dispensations,

1) Innocence (Prior to Adam)
2) Conscience (Adam to Noah)
3) Human Government (Noah to Abraham)
4) Promise or Patriarchal Rule (Abraham to Moses)
5) Mosaic Law (Moses to Christ)
6) Grace (the Church Age)
7) Kingdom (Millennium)

According to this scheme, we are living in the dispensation of Grace or the Church Age. Scofield explains,

> These periods are marked off in Scripture by some change in God's method of dealing with mankind, or a portion of mankind, in respect of the two questions: of sin, and of man's responsibility. Each of the Dispensations may be regarded as a new test of the natural man, and each ends in judgment—marking his utter failure. . . . We are living in the sixth, probably toward its close, and have before us the seventh, and last—the millennium. (Gaustad 1993:295)

Scofield listed not only seven dispensations but seven types of resurrections, eleven mysteries, eight covenants, two different comings of Christ, and a seven-year period of tribulation divided in half. As Martin Marty comments, "All students of his reference Bible could stay busy learning meanings that believers in eighteen Christian centuries had overlooked" (Marty 1986:220).

Counterpoint. However one chooses to slice up the Old Testament, no one doubts that there is development in the Bible. There is a progression from era to era as God's plan unfolds. The question is, toward what? Or should I say, toward whom? The New Testament reveals two dispensations: *promise and fulfillment*. Jesus Christ is the fulfillment, period.

The central motif of the New Testament is promise and fulfillment. This "hermeneutics of fulfillment" is the heart of the gospel. John the Baptist announced the nearness of God's salvation (see Chapter Five). Jesus then appeared and announced the arrival of the kingdom, the eschatological age of salvation fulfilled in himself. Paul wrote that all God's promises find their "yes" in Christ (2 Cor 1:20). The book of Hebrews declares that Christ is the mediator of "a better covenant which has been enacted through better promises" (Heb 8:6), that is, better than the earlier promises of the old dispensation.

Christian faith affirms that Jesus is the seed of Abraham, the Messiah, the Son of David, and the long-expected Savior. Jesus is what the Old Testament was anticipating. Thus, there are really two dispensations: promise and fulfillment. This brings us to the most controversial feature of dispensationalism, namely, the distinction between Israel and the church. Dispensationalists simply do not understand the New Testament doctrine of the church. If they did, they could never hold a two covenant theory of salvation.

5. The distinction between Israel and the church. The center of dispensationalism is the distinction between Israel and the church based on the two covenant theories of salvation. This presupposition drives the dispensational interpretation of scripture. It is traceable to Darby and was systematized by Scofield. Clarence Bass writes, "John Darby admits that it was a new truth that dawned upon him as a part of the development of his thought" (Bass 1960:26).

Darby taught that God's promises to ancient Israel are still binding, unconditional, and yet to be literally fulfilled. Meanwhile, the church is an unexpected interruption in God's plan, unforeseen in the Old Testament. The church is a parenthesis in a larger plan. Israel rejected Jesus, but those who believed in him became the church. Apparently, this was a surprise to God, so he had to revise his plan! After saving the church, God must deal with literal Israel and make good on his promises of old. This means juggling Bible prophecies,

- No Old Testament prophecy relates to the church, only to literal Israel.
- Israel and the church are two parallel peoples with two parallel destinies.
- Once the Church Age is finished (at the Rapture), God will begin fulfilling his promises to Israel.
- These promises will be fulfilled in the millennium, a one-thousand years Jewish kingdom under the rule of King Jesus.

Counterpoint. What is the relationship between Israel and the church? Does the church replace Israel? Is the church the new Israel? Is the church the new people of God?

Let's start with the early church. The first Christians were Jews who believed that Jesus was the Messiah. They were still part of Israel. They did not view their faith in Jesus as incompatible with Judaism. They viewed Jesus as the fulfillment of God's plan of redemption, as the Messiah. They certainly did not see themselves as a "parenthesis" in God's plan. These Jewish Christians saw themselves as the true Israel. The self-consciousness of the early church was hammered out in the crucible of conflict with Pharisaic Judaism. Hans Kung states, "This community [Christians] realized more and more clearly that through faith in Jesus as the Messiah it was the *true* Israel, the *true* people of God" (Kung 1967:119).

The question then arose, what happens to the "old" people of God? If the church is the new Israel "according to the Spirit," what happens to Israel "according to the flesh" (1 Cor 10:18)? If the church is the people of God, are the Jews still the people of God? Yes, but *conditionally*. This is the New Testament view.

The rupture between unbelieving Israel and the church widened. Paul refers to Israel "according to the flesh," meaning natural, unbelieving Israel (1 Cor 10:18). He says Christians are ministers of a new covenant superior to Moses (2 Cor 3). Christians are the true "circumcision" who worship God in the Spirit and place no confidence in Jewish pedigree (Phil 3:3-4). Not all members of literal Israel are true Israelites (Rom 9:6). Jews and Gentiles who believe in Christ are Abraham's children and heirs to the promises (Rom 4; Gal 3). Paul views the church as fulfilling the true destiny of Israel through faith in Jesus the Messiah, and he carries sorrow in his heart for those Jews who persist in unbelief (Rom 9:1-3). A remnant of Jews will yet believe, however. This is Paul's hope (Rom 11). But Paul never gives any indication that the Old Testament promises to Israel will be literally fulfilled in the distant future after the Rapture. Paul, in fact, didn't teach the Rapture.

In First Peter we are told that Christians are "a chosen race, a royal priesthood, a holy nation, God's own people" (1 Pt 2:9). A straightforward reading of these words concludes that the church is the new people of God. But perhaps the best book in the New Testament about this subject is Hebrews. The letter to the Hebrews is grounded in the belief that Jesus is the fulfillment of Old Testament types and the church is the new people of God. Hebrews chapter 11 lists the great heroes of faith in the Old Testament, but then concludes,

> Yet all these, though they were commended for their faith, did not receive what was promised, since God had provided something better so that they would not, apart from us, be made perfect. (Heb 11:39)

Apart from us! The connection between the old and new is now complete. The old has been fulfilled in the new. Hebrews declares to believers, "You have come to Mount Zion and to the city of the living God, the heavenly Jerusalem . . ." (Heb 12:22). There is no doubt that the New Testament views the church as the fulfillment of the promises made to ancient Israel. There is no basis in the New Testament for the dispensational view that the church is a parenthesis in God's plan and that the Old Testament prophecies regarding Israel must be literally fulfilled at some future date.

6. The Pretribulation Rapture. The Rapture removes the church from history before the Tribulation. It is for Christians only. The unbelieving world is "left behind." Following the Rapture, there are seven years of terrible times while Christians observe from heaven.

The Rapture was Darby's way of removing the church from earth so that God could refocus on fulfilling his promises to ancient Israel. God is busy during the Tribulation fulfilling Old Testament prophecies. Dispensationalists believe that Revelation 6-19 describes the Tribulation *with no church present on earth.* Dispensationalism teaches a two-phase coming of Christ. The Rapture is the first phase. After the Tribulation, Christ will return in glory to fight the battle of Armageddon and set up the millennial kingdom.

Counterpoint. Prior to the nineteenth century the Rapture was never taught. Furthermore, belief in the Rapture is not rooted in sound biblical exegesis but in the dispensational distinction between Israel and the church. Ecclesiology drives Rapture theology. This is made clear in a stunning admission by John Walvoord,

> It is safe to say that pretribulationism depends on a particular definition of the church . . . If the term *church* includes saints of all ages, then it is self-evident that the church will go through the Tribulation, as all agree that there will be saints in this time of trouble. If, however, the term *church* applies only to a certain body of saints, namely, the saints of this present dispensation, then the possibility of the translation of the church before the Tribulation is possible and even probable. (Walvoord 1979:21-22)

In other words, if a person adheres to sound biblical exegesis regarding Israel and the church, there is no need to believe in the Rapture! But if a person is a dispensationalist, then the Rapture is "possible," even "probable." Belief in the Rapture is an outcome of a dispensationalist view of the church. There is no biblical evidence to support the Rapture. *None*. Various passages are cited, but all these refer to the second coming, not the Rapture. A popular passage is 1 Thessalonians 4:13-18. Paul writes,

> For the Lord himself, with a cry of command, with the archangel's call and with the sound of God's trumpet, will descend from heaven, and the dead in Christ will rise first. Then we who are alive, who are left, will be caught up in the clouds together with them to meet the Lord in the air.

In what way is Paul describing a "secret" Rapture? Cry of command? Archangel's call? Sound of God's trumpet? Paul is embellishing on the Roman practice of the Emperor coming to town. It's a royal procession. There is nothing secret about it. This passage is describing the public and visible second coming of Christ (see Chapter Thirteen). It is not a Rapture passage.

Other supposedly Rapture texts are John 14:1-3 and 1 Corinthians 15:51-52. But again, these texts are dealing with the second coming of Christ, unless someone has a premeditated dispensational agenda. Tim LaHaye lists twenty-four New Testament passages that allegedly describe the Rapture, but in fact each one refers to the second coming (LaHaye 1999:99). The only way to get the Rapture from Bible is to misinterpret the Bible. Dispensationalism is based on faulty exegesis.

Doomsday for Darbyism?

We have discussed six main features of dispensational theology,

- Inerrancy
- Consistent literalism
- Futurist premillennialism
- Dispensations
- The distinction between Israel and the Church
- The pretribulation Rapture

These are traceable to John Nelson Darby. As I said earlier, dispensationalism is the eschatology of Christian fundamentalism. It is a method of interpreting Bible prophecy in a literal manner that results in an exotic understanding of Israel and the church. But is Darbyism a plausible theology in the long run?

First, dispensationalism is not the only form of premillennialism. Seventh-day Adventists, for example, are premillennial but reject dispensationalism. Most evangelicals are premillennial but are not dispensationalists; this includes Billy Graham. Second, dispensationalism is a jonnie-come-lately to Christian eschatology. This doesn't automatically imply error, but it is a fact that dispensationalism is a controversial new kid on the block that is incompatible with historic Christian eschatology.

Finally, the real issue is hermeneutics, or the interpretation of scripture. The greatest threat to dispensationalism is sound biblical exegesis. Clarence Bass notes that dispensationalism is based "on a faulty hermeneutical basis of interpretation" (1960:155). Can dispensationalism bear the strain of "consistent literalism" when that very literalism lacks credibility? Can dispensationalists continue their blind support for Israel and remain credible? Can dispensationalists weather the storm created by their own misguided prophets who keep predicting the Rapture and setting dates for the end?

The most pressing issue facing dispensationalism today is plausibility. Someday we mght look back on dispensationalism as just another chapter in Christianity's wacky eschatological landscape, like the Fifth Monarchy men in 17th century England or the Millerites in 19th century America. So much passion and conviction, but where are they now? Left behind.

Our next chapter will show that dispensationalism is more than eschatological fantasies; it is a political theology called "Christian Zionism." Here is where a theology of the last days becomes dangerous.

20

Romancing Israel: Christian Zionism Today

Christian Zionists love Israel. It is a romance.

From ecstasy about "the regathering of the Jews" to breathless excitement about the rebuilding of the Jewish temple, Christian Zionists ride on the waves of Bible prophecies that are allegedly being fulfilled every day. Christian fundamentalists and evangelicals tour the Holy Land, often guided by right-wing Jewish extremists who have a political agenda. "This is our land! God promised it to Abraham! The Palestinians have no right to be here! Someday we will reclaim the Temple Mount from the Muslims!"

Love is blind. This applies to Christian Zionists and their love affair with Israel.

Is the state of Israel the fulfillment of Bible prophecy? Does the entire land of Palestine belong to the Jews? Should the Palestinians leave? Will the Jewish temple be rebuilt before the Messiah arrives? Should Christians be pro-Israel and send money to Israel in order to fund more illegal Jewish settlements? Will the Jews ultimately be converted to Christ? Does the Bible teach that Christ will literally descend to Jerusalem and set up his millennial kingdom in the Holy City?

These beliefs are part of Christian Zionist theology, which is also right-wing political ideology. The romance with Israel has three pillars: (1) the reestablishment of the Jewish nation; (2) the gathering of the Jews to their homeland; (3) the rebuilding of the Jewish temple on the Temple Mount. Christian Zionists believe the Bible predicts all these things happening before the end. Of course, these three events are merely a prelude to the great Battle of Armageddon. Christian Zionism is a constellation of convictions about events leading up to the end of the world.

But romance must be grounded in reality. Stubborn facts remain. All the "candlelight dinners" between Christian Zionists and Israeli hard liners cannot make the world go away. There needs to be a critique. Is Christian Zionism Christian? Is it not misguided zeal based on a faulty theology?

I believe Christian Zionists are wrong and that their theology is dangerous. Christian Zionism is the logical outcome of dispensationalism. The ultimate agenda of Christian Zionists is the conversion of the Jews and the official end of the Jewish faith. Let's get to the heart of this type of thinking.

Zionist Fever in Texas

Pastor John Hagee is the Founder and National Chairman of Christians United for Israel (CUFI), a pro-Israel group of conservative Christians that was formed in February 2006. CUFI's motto is Isaiah 62:1, *"For Zion's sake I will not keep silent, and for Jerusalem's sake I will not rest, until her vindication shines out like the dawn, and her salvation like a burning torch."* Another key verse is God's promise to Abraham,

> Go from your country and your kindred and your father's house to the land that I will show you. I will make of you

> a great nation, and I will bless you, and make your name great, so that you will be a blessing. I will bless those who bless you, and the one who curses you I will curse; and in you all the families of the earth shall be blessed. (Gen 12:3)

Commenting on the above verses, the CUFI website says, "These and so many other verses of the Bible have one overriding message—as Christians we have a Biblical obligation to defend Israel and the Jewish people in their time of need" (www.cufi.org). The purpose of CUFI is "to provide a national association through which every pro-Israel church, parachurch organization, ministry or individual in America can speak and act with one voice in support of Israel in matters related to Biblical issues."

Pastor Hagee is a dispensationalist who has written a number of prophecy books, including *Jerusalem Countdown: A Warning to the World* (2006). In that book, Hagee makes his position on Israel very clear,

> Jerusalem is the heart of Israel. There are voices now calling for the sacred city to be shared as part of the Roadmap for Peace in the Middle East. Let it be known to all men far and near, the city of Jerusalem is not up for negotiation with anyone at any time for any reason in the future. It has been and shall always be the eternal and undivided capital of the State of Israel. (Hagee 2006:49-50)

Hagee's church, Cornerstone Church in San Antonio, Texas, has almost 18,000 members. Religion blends with politics at Cornerstone, and the politics are conservative, Republican, and enthusiastically Zionist. Church members who wish to donate money in support of Israel sign a pledge card stating, "I want to be a part of the fulfillment of prophecy and the courageous effort to return Jewish families to their homeland." According to Timothy P. Weber,

Hagee claims to have raised $3.7 million in order to relocate over six thousand Jews to Israel (Weber 2004:227).

Christian Zionists claim that their support of Israel is not linked to end-times prophecies. Rather, it is based on sound Bible truth regarding Israel. Hagee states, "We do not support Israel for any end-times scenario. We support Israel for Bible reasons that have been there for 2,000 years" (Flakus 2008). Yet Hagee's eschatology is dispensationalist, his view of the end of the world is dispensationalist, his distinction between Israel and the church is dispensationalist, his understanding of the Rapture, the Tribulation, and the Battle of Armageddon is dispensationalist. Frankly, it is difficult *not* to view Christian Zionism as dispensationalist political theology and intimately related to an end-times script. Christian Zionists view the nation Israel as the fulfillment of Bible prophecy, and this view is a central pillar of dispensationalism. Contrary to what Hagee claims, his support of Israel is directly tied to an "end-times scenario."

Can we ignore the implications of this theology for U.S. foreign policy? In November 2009, conservative lightning rod, Sarah Palin, was interviewed by ABC news. When asked about her religious beliefs, she affirmed her dispensationalist, pro-Israel theology. She supports the continual expansion of Jewish settlements in the West Bank, even though such settlements contradict international law. Regarding Jews returning to their homeland, she stated, "More and more Jewish people will be flocking to Israel in the days and weeks and months ahead." This is an odd claim, since Jewish immigration to Israel is declining (Olbermann 2009).

We must seriously ask what might happen when Bible prophecy drives foreign policy. This is the politics of Armageddon.

The Geopolitics of Christian Zionism

We believe God gave the land to the descendents of Israel. It was not given to Palestine, it wasn't given to so-called Palestinians.

—*Pat Robertson*

Not all Jews welcome the enthusiasm of Christian Zionists. In April 2008, Rabbi Eric Yoffie, president of the 1.5 million member Reform Judaism movement, called Pastor Hagee an "extremist" and accused Hagee of fostering religious intolerance. Yoffie said, "Their vision of Israel rejects a two-state solution, rejects the possibility of a democratic Israel, and supports the permanent occupation of all Arab territory now controlled by Israel" (Christian Century 2008).

In a PBS interview with Bill Moyers in autumn 2007, Rabbi Michael Lerner lamented the extremism of Christian Zionists. He noted that the pro-Israel movement among evangelicals aligns itself with the most radical and dangerous elements in Israeli politics. Lerner asserts, "The Christian Zionists are really an important element in the Israel lobby today, pushing the United States towards support of the most conservative and unloving policies" (Moyers 2007).

Clearly there is trouble in the Christian Zionist camp. Tony Campolo, an evangelical leader, views Christian Zionism as "the most dangerous influence of dispensationalism" on American policies toward Israel. Christian Zionists, he asserts, "have become a major barrier, if not *the* major barrier, to peace in the Middle East" (Campolo 2005). In late August 2006, the Vatican and three other Christian bodies signed a document entitled "Jerusalem Declaration on Christian Zionism" that was nothing less than a frontal assault on the Christian Zionist movement. It said in part, "We reject the teachings of Christian Zionism that facilitate and support those policies as they advance racial exclusivity and perpetual war" (Tostevin 2006).

In the dispensationalist scheme of geopolitics, Israel is the most important nation in the world; without Israel the whole system falls apart. The logic of dispensationalism leads inevitably to an uncritical pro-Israel stance and an "Israel-is-always-right" approach to foreign policy. Genesis 15:18 states, "On that day the Lord made a covenant with Abram, saying, 'To your descendants I give this land, from the river of Egypt to the great river, the river Euphrates.'" Taken literally, this means that Israel should rightfully occupy a region extending from the Nile River in Egypt to Iraq! Christian Zionists support Israel because they believe God gave the land to the Jews and that Bible prophecies about Israel must be literally fulfilled. Talk of "land for peace" goes against God's plan.

In 2003, television evangelist Pat Robertson said,

> We believe God gave the land to the descendents of Israel. It was not given to Palestine, it wasn't given to so-called Palestinians. It wasn't given to Saudis or the Syrians. It was given to the descendents of Abraham, Isaac and Jacob through Joshua. This has been the land of Israel. And it belongs to them. And God is not going to let anybody take it away from them. (www.patrobertson.com)

Hagee and other Christian Zionists create a rigid dualism between all-out support of Israel and no support. There are no gray areas or room for compromise. How can someone compromise on the word of God? If God said the land belongs to the Jews, then the land belongs to the Jews! This is why Christian Zionism has aligned itself with the most extreme right-wing Jewish Zionists.

Christian Zionists have worked hard to influence American foreign policy regarding Israel. In 2006, the Bush administration convened a series of off-the-record meetings regarding Middle East policy with leaders of Christians United for Israel (CUFI). According to CUFI, support for Israel's expansionist policies is "a biblical imperative" (Blumenthal 2006). CUFI pressed the White House to be more confrontational with Iran, to stop aid to the Palestinians, and to allow Israel a free hand in being more aggressive toward Hezbollah, an Islamic terrorist organization. Daniel Pipes has written, "To those who wonder why Washington follows policies so different from the European states, a large part of the answer these days has to do with the clout of Christian Zionists, who are especially powerful when a conservative Republican like George W. Bush is president" (Pipes 2003).

It is becoming clear to many religious and political leaders that Christian Zionism is a barrier to peace in the Middle East. Jews themselves resent the implication that eventually they are expected to accept Jesus as the Messiah or else be annihilated with the rest of the wicked. The logic of Christian Zionism is a paradox for Jews: "We love you and support you, but if you don't accept Christ, you will be destroyed." As Dan Cohn-Sherbok states in *Tikkun* magazine, "The paradox of this Jewish-Christian alliance is that Christian Zionist theology envisages the ultimate disappearance of Judaism as a living religion" (Cohn-Sherbok 2008).

What about those promises of land in the Old Testament? Are they relevant to Christians anymore? Is the fate of the world dependent on a literal interpretation of Bible prophecies related to the Holy Land? Hans Kung writes,

> Can one here and now, with reference to the Bible, lay down specific political frontiers and make quite specific territorial demands? ... As if the present-day Arab and Muslim inhabitants, who have been settled here for around 1200 years, did not possess any legitimate rights to a home and could even be deported!" (Kung 1992:559-61)

I can understand why the land is important to Jews. Jewish theology is grounded in election, covenant, land, and messianic hope. We can respect this and embrace a partial appreciation for it, but are Christians called to support it? Are Christians called to join the fracas and help Israel repossess the land? Where is such a mandate found in the New Testament? The Christian Zionist romance with the land of Israel is based on Old Testament prophecies interpreted literally, as if the New Testament had never been written.

The theological framework of Christian Zionism is fatally flawed. Step back and consider the central assumption of Christianity: the New Covenant. This New Covenant is based on God's action in Jesus the Messiah and is founded on the death and resurrection of Christ. The New Covenant makes the Old Covenant obsolete; it both fulfills and supersedes what preceded it. Hebrews says, "He abolishes the first in order to establish the second" (10:9). Furthermore, the church is a worldwide spiritual community without a physical homeland. The issue of land is superfluous. The gospel transcends a theology of land.

Add to this the ideas of exile and pilgrimage. Christians are exiles on earth, dispersed throughout the world (1 Pt 1:1). The people of God is a pilgrim people in search of a better country, "a heavenly one," based on better promises (Heb 11:13-16). I have found no text in the New Testament calling for Christians to support a "holy war" for land. That might be a Jewish idea, but it is not a Christian idea. When Christian Zionists embrace the Israeli far-right, they are forming an alliance that the majority of Jews reject, as well as going beyond the bounds of historic Christian faith.

The Politics of Sacred Space

I am concerned that if there is an explosion here, it will spill across the world.

-- Mohammed Tamimi, overseer of the Temple Mount

We now move from land to sacred space: the Temple Mount in Jerusalem. Christian Zionism supports the literal rebuilding of the temple in Jerusalem on the Temple Mount, even though the site is occupied by Muslims.

Solomon's temple was destroyed by the Babylonians in 587 B.C. The Second Temple, started around 515 B.C., was destroyed by the Romans in 70 A.D. Since then Jews have been without a literal temple. Synagogue worship replaced temple worship and rabbis replaced priests. Many Jews hope and pray for a "third temple" to be built before the coming of the Messiah. This is an eschatological hope. Rebuilding the temple is tied to the Messiah's arrival. Israel must *desire* to rebuild the temple more fervently. Otherwise, the Messiah's arrival will be delayed. But by desiring enough and by taking steps to get the job done, Jews can hasten the Messianic Age.

Christian Zionists share these beliefs. They fully support "the Temple Mount" movement. Here, they believe, is where Jesus will come when he returns in glory. Here also is where religion and politics could lead to a wide scale international conflict.

The Temple Mount is the third holiest place in Islam and is known as the Noble Sanctuary. It is the place where the angel Gabriel brought Muhammad to embark on his ascent to heaven to visit with other prophets. The Dome of the Rock and the Al-Aqsa Mosque now dominate the space where the Jewish temple once stood. The temple complex is the most incendiary 35 acres of real estate in the world. Five hundred persons are employed to staff the holy site. Jordan functions as the overseer, according to a controversial agreement following the Six-Day War (1967). Since 1969, there have been twelve efforts to destroy the Temple Mount or to kill Muslims in the area. One of the radicals, Yehuda Etzion, was convicted of planning the failed attack of January 26, 1984. He said, "Four years ago I began to contemplate the necessity to purify the Temple Mount from the grip of Islam" (Kimball 2002:100).

Muslims are continually on high alert, suspecting a Jewish takeover of the Temple Mount. Clashes between Muslims and Jews are cyclical. Riots broke out in October 2009, around the time of Yom Kippur. "Temple temptations" are irresistible for Jewish extremists; Muslim radicals are also looking for a chance at retaliation. Mohammed Tamimi directs the Jerusalem Waqf, and oversees the Temple compound on Jordan's behalf. He says, "For those who want to stir up trouble, it is not difficult. I am concerned that if there is an explosion here, it will spill across the world" (Schneider 2009).

The temple has eschatological significance for radical Jews. God's program, they believe, cannot move forward until steps are taken to reclaim the Temple Mount and rebuild the temple. According the website of The Temple Institute in Jerusalem, "Geopolitically, the Temple Mount has to be cleared of the Dome of the Rock and the mosques which are presently located upon it before the physical rebuilding of the Holy Temple can begin" (www.templeinstitute.org).

The Temple Institute has been preparing sacred vessels and vestments for use in the restored temple. "These vessels and priestly garments are being fashioned today according to the exact Biblical requirements, specifically for use in the future Holy Temple. They await the day when they will be called into the Divine service of the Holy Temple" (www.templeinstitute.org).

American dispensationalists regularly visit the Temple Institute while touring the Holy Land. By some accounts, over one-hundred thousand visitors per year view the institute's displays of sacred vessels and vestments. Sixty percent of the visitors are non-Jews. "Without the evangelical tourists, it is doubtful that the institute could carry on its many programs. Dispensationalists are thrilled to see what is going on, since the plan fits well with their own expectations for the end" (Weber 2004:261). Christian Zionists are more than willing to contribute money—lots of it—to the Temple project. This is one way to support God's plan for Israel, according to Bible prophecies.

I ask again, what has this to do with Christian theology? Has Christian Zionism missed the memo regarding the temple in the New Testament?

Jesus predicted the destruction of the temple (Matt 24:1-2). He pointed to his death as the end of the temple services (Jn 2:19-22). Early on, Jewish Christians still focused on the temple, but this changed as the mission to the Gentiles became clearer and Christianity moved into the Greco-Roman world. The book of Acts traces this journey. One of the earliest spokespersons of this view was Stephen, who was martyred for his attack on the temple and the Mosaic Law: "The Most High does not dwell in houses made with human hands" (Acts 7:48). Ephesians views the church itself as God's new temple, "with Christ Jesus himself as the cornerstone" (Eph 2:20). Even the book of Revelation describes the New Jerusalem without a temple: "I saw no temple in the city, for its temple is the Lord God the Almighty and the Lamb" (Rev 21:22).

From Jewish sect to worldwide religion—this has been the history of Christianity. That the Jewish temple must be literally rebuilt before the coming of the Lord is a foreign idea to the New Testament. There is absolutely nothing Christian about it.

The End of Romance

They say that breaking up is hard to do; now I know,
I know that it's true.

--Neil Sedaka, hit song

Breaking up is hard to do, as the old song says. It is especially hard in regard to religion. Changing a religious position can create psychic trauma. One's worldview crumbles and what is left? One can become an outcast or a pariah, or worse yet, a total heretic facing certain damnation.

The fate of Christian Zionism is tied to dispensationalism, and there are no signs that dispensationalism is going away. An entire publishing market is based on dispensationalist theology: the Rapture, the Tribulation, the Antichrist, the rebuilding of the Jewish temple, Armageddon, and an earthly millennial kingdom.

Christian Zionists assume that things will get worse and worse. All this is "predicted" by Bible prophecy, which grinds along on its predestined course. It's called fatalism. As long as doomsday prophets embrace theological fatalism in the abstract, there is no problem. We can let them do their own thing quietly on the sidelines. But when dispensational fatalism becomes proactive and political, dubious Bible prophecies become self-fulfilling. Well-meaning Christians can find themselves on the side of world destruction. The romance with Armageddon becomes deadly.

Christians Zionists pose one of the greatest threats to reasonable world peace. They do not help the peace process because they are not interested in peace. They seem willing to sacrifice the entire human race in order to see Bible prophecies come true. This is where eschatology becomes dangerous to the human race.

Epilogue: God the Finisher

The whole is oriented to that last end of ends, which we call God, in fact God the Finisher.

--Hans Kung

I am writing this final chapter on New Year's Day 2012. According to the Mayan calendar, this is the year the world enters a new Cosmic Age. Whether or not this is the case, even the Mayans have their eschatology. In fact, the great religions of the world are eschatological and are driven toward "the beyond," the ultimate destiny of human beings. John Hick describes the eschatological character of Buddhism and Hinduism, as well as Judaism, Christianity, and Islam. Hick views these religions as systems of salvation or liberation that proclaim "a limitlessly better possibility arising from another reality, transcendent to our present selves" (Hick 2004:56). We might call it "cosmic optimism." Therefore, it is not wishful thinking to be optimistic about 2012. Optimism is the nature of religious faith that is grounded in God. The words of the Christian mystic, Julian of Norwich, are appropriate here,

"All shall be well,
and all shall be well,
and all manner of things shall be well."

As finite beings, we are driven toward the infinite. As limited beings, we are driven toward the limitless. As mortal beings, we are driven toward immortality. Eschatology is the passion for the infinite, because the infinite has grasped us and won't let us go. It is the conviction of every religion that the best things in life are eternal things, and that our lives are enhanced by affirming the eternal within time—the Eternal Now. Religion is the human response to the power of the infinite that is already in us. This is why religion is incurably eschatological; it leans into the future, into God who is our final destiny: *God the Finisher.*

Christian eschatology is about the completion of God's purpose for creation and history. It is eschatology grounded in scripture, in the revelation of God through Israel, Jesus Christ, and the New Testament. We discovered the need to translate the biblical images of the end into a modern idiom; we need to demythologize the biblical myths (most of them apocalyptic). We can talk about the end only in images and pictures, or stories and myths. Rather than repudiate such mythology, it needs to be reinterpreted. But the fundamental conviction behind all Christian eschatology is belief in *God the Finisher.* As Hans Kung writes, "Both at the beginning of the world, and at its end, there is not nothing, but God" (Kung 1980:656). Thus, Christian faith views the end not as annihilation but completion and fulfillment. Christian faith leans into final fulfillment: the consummation.

How or when the consummation will occur is a mystery. The biblical images of the end are not play-by-play descriptions of coming events. Doomsday theology interprets literally what is meant to be understood metaphorically, and this is why it is wrong-headed. Nevertheless, Christian faith is confidence in God the Finisher to bring to completion his purpose for creation and humanity. According to the Book of Common Prayer 1979,

> The Christian hope is to live with confidence in newness and fullness of life, and to await the coming of Christ in glory, and the completion of God's purpose for the world. (BCP 861)

Confident living while we wait for God to complete his purpose for the world—this is a brief summary of Christian hope. What is our assurance? The Prayer Book addresses this,

> Our assurance as Christians is that nothing, not even death, shall separate us from the love of God which is in Christ Jesus our Lord. Amen. (BCP 862)

We live with confidence in newness and fullness of life, and in hope of God's coming future. We live with the assurance that nothing will ever separate us from God's eternal love.

This book has emphasized that Christians live between the times. We live between "the already and the not yet." God is already present with us, his kingdom exerts its saving influence here and now, and people are doing the work of God throughout the world here and now. Every day of the year, including this year, people are responding to God's grace and doing God's work here and now. As Jesus said, "You are the salt of the earth . . . you are the light of the world" (Matt 5:13-14). God has not abandoned the world to evil, and God's people are called to resist evil and do good while time lasts.

Yet we must not lose sight of God's coming future and our ultimate destiny in God. Jesus said the poor in spirit will enter the kingdom of heaven, those who mourn will be comforted, the meek will inherit the earth, those who hunger for justice will be satisfied, the merciful will receive mercy, the pure in heart will see God, the peacemakers will be called children of God, and those who are persecuted will be rewarded with a place in the kingdom (Matt 5:3-10). These promises are future-oriented. The fullness of salvation awaits us. The kingdom of God is present only fragmentarily. We hunger for completion and final resolution to the problems of sin, evil, and suffering. We can experience the love and mercy of God now, yet we have not achieved the full vision of God.

Christian hope is hope in God the Finisher. It is *fundamental trust in reality*, saying yes to God, God's world, and God's future. This is the essence of Christian eschatology, and this is why I am optimistic about 2012. In the end, there is not nothing; there is God the Finisher.

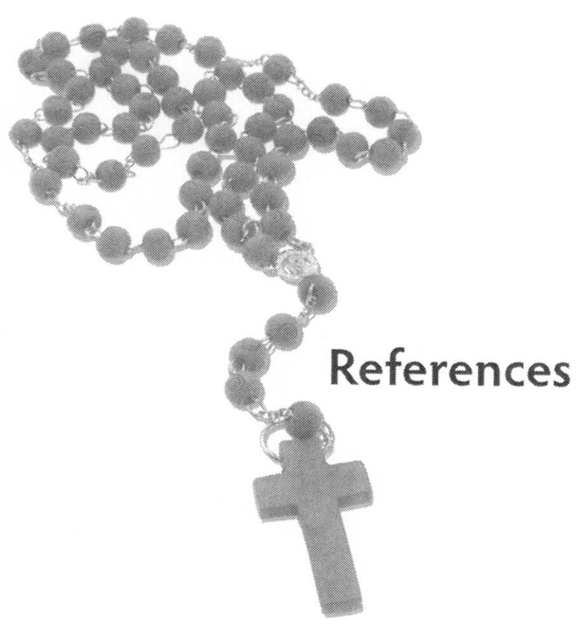

References

Preface

Waits, J. (2011). "Harold Camping Issues Vague Apology, Says World will End without Warning." Radio Survivor Website. Retrieved November 29, 2011, from http://www.radiosurvivor.com/2011/11/02/harold-camping-issues-vague-apology-says-world-will-end-without-warning/

Chapter One: Eschatology for Dummies

Tillich, P. (1967). *A History of Christian Thought*. Ed. Carl E. Braaten. New York: Simon Schuster.

Chapter Two: God in History?

Dodd, C. H. (1960). *The Authority of the Bible*. Glasgow: Fontana Books.

Jewitt, R. & Lawrence, J. S. (2003). *Captain America and the*

Crusade against Evil. Grand Rapids, MI: Wm. B. Eerdmans Publishing Company.

Moltmann, J. (1991). *Theology of Hope.* Minneapolis, MN: Fortress Press.

Pannenberg, W. (1998). *Systematic Theology.* 3 vols. Grand Rapids, MI: Wm. B. Eerdmans Publishing Co.

Rist, M. (1962). Apocalypticism. *The Interpreter's Dictionary of the Bible.* Ed. George A. Buttrick. Nashville: Abingdon Press. 5 Vols. 1:157-161.

Chapter Three: Reading Daniel with One Eye Squinted

Collins, John J. (2005). "Apocalypse: Jewish Apocalypticism to the Rabbinic Period." *Encyclopedia of Religion.* Ed. Lindsay Jones. 2nd ed. Vol. 1. Detroit, MI: Macmillan Reference USA. 1:414-419. *Gale Virtual Reference Library.* Retrieved January 17, 2011.

Frost, Stanley. B. (1962). "Daniel." *Interpreter's Dictionary of the Bible.* Ed. George A. Buttrick. Nashville, TN: Abingdon Press. 5 vols. 1:761-68.

Gottwald, Norman K. (1985). *The Hebrew Bible: A Socio-Literary Introduction.* Philadelphia, PA: Fortress Press.

Hartman, Louis F. & Di Lella, Alexander A. (1978). *The Book of Daniel. Vol.* 23. The Anchor Bible Commentary. Garden City, NY: Doubleday & Company, Inc.

Von Rad, Gerhard. (1965). *Old Testament Theology.* Trans. D. M. G. Stalker. 2 vols. New York: Harper & Row, Publishers.

Chapter Four: Messianic Hope in Judaism

Aran, G. (1991). Jewish Zionist Fundamentalism. *Fundamentalisms Observed.* Ed. M. E. Marty & R. S. Appleby. Chicago: University of Chicago Press. Pp. 265-344.

Ariel, D. S. (1995). *What Do Jews Believe?* New York: Schocken.

Finkel, A. Y. (Ed.). (1994). *The Essential Maimonides.* Northvale, NJ: Jason Aronson Inc.

Jenni, E. (1962). Messiah, Jewish. *Interpreter's Dictionary of the Bible.* Ed. George A. Buttrick. Nashville, TN: Abingdon Press. 5 Vols. 3:360-365.

Kung, H. (1993). *Judaism: Between Yesterday and Tomorrow.* New York: Crossroad.

Lerner, M. (1994). *Jewish Renewal: A Path to Healing and Transformation.* New York: HarperPerennial.

Moltmann, J. (1990). *The Way of Jesus Christ.* Minneapolis, MN: Fortress Press.

Werblowsky, R. J. Zwi (1987). Messianism. *Contemporary Jewish Religious Thought.* Ed. A. A. Cohen & P. Mendes-Flohr. New York: Charles Scribner's Sons. Pp. 597-602.

Chapter Five: Jesus and John the Baptist

Bornkamm, G. (1960). *Jesus of Nazareth.* New York: Harper & Row Publishers.

Crossan, J. D. (1994). *Jesus: A Revolutionary Biography.* New York: HarperCollins Publishers.

Klausner, J. (1964). *Jesus of Nazareth: His Life, Times, and Teaching.* Boston: Beacon Press.

Moltmann, J. (1993). *The Way of Jesus Christ.* Minneapolis, MN: Fortress Press.

Chapter Six: Did Jesus Believe in the End of the World?

Bornkamm, G. (1960). *Jesus of Nazareth.* New York: Harper & Row Publishers.

Ehrman, B. (1999). *Jesus: Apocalyptic Prophet of the New Millennium.* New York: Oxford University Press.

Ehrman, B. (2000). *The New Testament: A Historical Introduction to the Early Christian Writings*. 2nd ed. New York: Oxford University Press.

Kung, H. (1976). *On Being a Christian*. New York: Doubleday.

Moltmann, J. (1993). *The Way of Jesus Christ*. Minneapolis, MN: Fortress Press.

Schillebeeckx, E. (1979). *Jesus: An Experiment in Christology*. New York: Seabury Press.

Schweitzer. A. (1998). *The Quest of the Historical Jesus*. Baltimore, MD: The Johns Hopkins University Press.

Sanders, E. P. (1993). *The Historical Figure of Jesus*. London: Penguin Books.

Chapter Seven: Mark 13: Soon, But Not That Soon

Gager, J. G. (1975). *Kingdom and Community: The Social World of Early Christianity*. Englewood Cliffs, NJ: Prentice-Hall, Inc.

Chapter Eight: Jesus and Ethics: Is Love Really Enough?

Bornkamm, G. (1960). *Jesus of Nazareth*. New York: Harper & Row Publishers.

Bultmann, R. (1958). *Jesus and the Word*. New York: Charles Scribner's Sons.

Crook, R. H. (2002). *Introduction to Christian Ethics*. 4th ed. Upper Saddle River, NJ: Prentice Hall

Ehrman, B. D. (1999). *Jesus: Apocalyptic Prophet of the New Millennium*. New York: Oxford University Press.

Kung, H. (1978). *On Being A Christian*. New York: Doubleday.

Niebuhr, R. (1979). *An Interpretation of Christian Ethics*. New York: The Seabury Press.

Ramsey, P. (1993). *Basic Christian Ethics*. Forward by Stanley

Hauerwas and D. Stephen Lang. Louisville, KY: Westminster/ John Knox Press.

Chapter Nine: The Cross as an Eschatological Event

Bornkamm, G. (1960). *Jesus of Nazareth.* New York: Harper and Row Publishers.

Kung, H. (1992). *Judaism: Between Yesterday and Tomorrow.* New York: Crossroad Publishing Co.

Moltmann, J. (1974, 1993). *The Crucified God.* Minneapolis, MN: Fortress Press.

Moltmann, (1990, 1993). *The Way of Jesus Christ.* Minneapolis, MN: Fortress Press.

Pannenberg, W. (1968, 2002). *Jesus—God and Man.* London: SCM Press.

Schillebeeckx, E. (1979). *Jesus: An Experiment in Christology.* New York: Seabury.

Senior, D. (1984). *The Passion of Jesus in the Gospel of Mark.* Wilmington, DE: Michael Glazier, Inc.

Chapter Ten: The Resurrection?

Borg, M. J. (2003). *The Heart of Christianity: Rediscovering a Life of Faith.* New York: HarperCollins.

Fredricksen, P. (2000). *From Jesus to Christ.* 2nd ed. New Haven: Yale University Press.

Moltmann, J. (1993). *The Way of Jesus Christ.* Minneapolis, MN: Fortress Press.

Rahner, K. (1978). *Foundations of Christian Faith.* New York: The Seabury Press.

Rahner, K. (1993). *The Content of Faith.* New York: Crossroad Publishing Co.

Chapter Eleven: John and the Church: Backing Off Apocalyptic

Tillich, P. (1955). *The New Being.* New York: Charles Scribner's Sons

Chapter Twelve: Pentecost

Kung, H. (1967). *The Church.* New York: Sheed and Ward.

Tillich, P. (1963). *Systematic Theology, Vol. 3.* Chicago: University of Chicago Press.

Chapter Thirteen: Rescue from Orion?

Ehrman, B. (2000). *The New Testament: A Historical Introduction to the Early Christian Writings.* 2nd ed. New York: Oxford University Press.

Kung, H. (1976). *On Being a Christian.* New York: Doubleday & Company, Inc.

McArthur, H. K. (1962). Parousia. *Interpreter's Dictionary of the Bible.* Ed. George A. Buttrick. Nashville, TN: Abingdon Press. 5 Vols. 3:658-661.

Moltmann, J.. (1996). *The Coming of God: Christian Eschatology.* Minneapolis: Fortress Press.

Chapter Fourteen: Paul and Israel

Bruce, F. F. (1977). *Paul: Apostle of the Heart Set Free.* Grand Rapids, MI: Wm. B. Eerdmans Publishing Co.

Chapter Fifteen: Hebrews and the Coming World

Ehrman, B. (2000). *The New Testament: A Historical Introduction to the Early Christian Writings.* New York: Oxford University Press.

Ladd, G. E. (1993). *A Theology of the New Testament.* Rev. ed. Grand Rapids, MI.: William B. Eerdmans Publishing Co.

Chapter Sixteen: Faithful Witnessing in the Book of Revelation

Bultmann, R. (1955). *Theology of the New Testament.* 2 Vols. Trans. by K. Grobel. New York: Charles Scribner's Sons.

Cohn, N. (1993). *Cosmos, Chaos, and the World to Come: The Ancient Roots of Apocalyptic Faith.* New Haven: Yale University Press.

Frend, W. H. C. (1984). *The Rise of Christianity.* Philadelphia: Fortress Press.

Metzger, B. (1993). *Breaking the Code: Understanding the Book of Revelation.* Nashville: Abingdon Press.

Moltmann, J. (2004). *In the End—the Beginning.* Minneapolis, MN: Fortress Press.

Perkins, P. (1988). *Reading the New Testament.* 2nd ed. Mahwah, NJ: Paulist Press.

Chapter Seventeen: Can the Millennium Be Salvaged?

Bauckham, R. & Hart, T. (1999). *Hope Against Hope: Christian Eschatology at the Turn of the Millennium.* Grand Rapids, MI: Wm. B. Eerdmans Publishing Co.

Erickson, M. J. (1977). *Contemporary Options in Eschatology: A Study of the Millennium.* Grand Rapids, MI: Baker Book House.

Grenz, S. J. (1992). *The Millennial Maze: Sorting Out Evangelical Options*. Downers Grove, IL: InterVarsity Press.

Oden, T. C. (1992). *Life in the Spirit. Systematic Theology: Volume Three*. Peabody, MA: Prince Press.

Pelikan, J. (1971). *The Emergence of the Catholic Tradition (100-600)*. Chicago: University of Chicago Press.

Rist, M. (1962). Millennium. *Interpreter's Dictionary of the Bible*. Ed. George A. Buttrick. Nashville, TN: Abingdon Press. 5 Vols. 3:381-82.

Turveson, L. T. (1968). *Redeemer Nation: The Idea of America's Millennial Role*. Chicago: University of Chicago Press.

Chapter Eighteen: Fellowship with the Dead?

Kung, H. (1993). *Credo: The Apostles' Creed Explained for Today*. New York: Doubleday.

Macquarrie, J. (1990). *Jesus Christ in Modern Thought*. London: SCM Press.

McNeill, J. T. (Ed.) (1960). *Calvin: Institutes of the Christian Religion*, 2 vols. Trans. by F. L. Battles. Library of Christian Classics Vols. XX and XXI. Philadelphia: Westminster Press.

Moltmann, J. (1990). *The Way of Jesus Christ*. Minneapolis: Fortress Press.

Moltmann, J. (1996). *The Coming of God*. Minneapolis: Fortress Press.

Moltmann, J. (2004). *In the End—The Beginning*. Minneapolis: Fortress Press.

Oden, T. C. (1992). *Life in the Spirit: Systematic Theology, Volume Three*. Peabody, MA.: Prince Press.

Chapter Nineteen: Left Behind? The Delusion of Dispensationalism

Barr, J. (1978). *Fundamentalism*. Philadelphia: Westminster Press.

Bass, C. B. (1960). *Backgrounds to Dispensationalism*. Grand Rapids, MI: Baker Book House.

Blaising, C. A. & Bock, D. L. (Eds.). (1992). *Dispensationalism, Israel, and the Church*. Grand Rapids, MI: Zondervan Publishing.

Gausted, E. S. (1993). (Ed.). *A Documented History of Religion in America since 1865*. 2nd ed. Grand Rapids, MI: Wm. B. Eerdmans Publishing, Co.

Kung, H. (1967). *The Church*. New York: Sheed and Ward.

LaHaye, T. & Jenkins, J. (1999). *Are We Living in the End Times?* Wheaton, IL: Tyndale House Publishers.

Marty, M. (1986). *Modern American Religion: The Irony of It All, 1893-1919*. 3 Vols. Chicago: University of Chicago Press.

Moyers, B. (2007, October 5). Interview on Christian Zionism with Dr. Timothy P. Weber and Rabbi Michael Lerner. Retrieved May 4, 2008 from www.pbs.org

Ryrie, C. C. (2007). *Dispensationalism*. Rev. ed. Chicago: Moody Publishers.

Walvoord, J. F. (1993). *The Final Drama: 14 Keys to Understanding the Prophetic Scriptures*. Grand Rapids, MI: Kregel Publications.

Walvoord, J. F. (1979). *The Rapture Question*. Rev. ed. Grand Rapids, MI: Zondervan.

Weber, T. P. (1998, October 5). How evangelicals became Israel's best friend. *Christianity Today* 42(11), 39+.

Weber, T. P. (1983). *Living in the Shadow of the Second Coming*. Grand Rapids, MI: Zondervan Publishing.

Chapter Twenty: Romancing Israel: Christian Zionism Today

Blumenthal, M. (2006, August 8). Birth pangs of a new Christian Zionism. Retrieved December 31, 2007, from http://www.thenation.com

Campolo, T. (2005, Jan/Feb). The ideological roots of Christian

Zionism [Electronic Version]. *Tikkun* 20(1), 19+. Retrieved October, 21, 2006, from ProQuest database.

Christian Century (2008, May 8). Reform Jewish leader calls Hagee 'extremist' unworthy of support. Retrieved May 12, 2008, from www.christiancentury.org

Flakus, G. (2008). US Christian Evangelicals Lend Support to Israel. Retrieved May 11, 2008, from http://www.voanews.com/english/2008-05-08-voa37.cfm

Hagee, J. (2006). *Jerusalem Countdown: A Warning to the World.* Lake Mary, FL: FrontLine.

Kimball, C. (2002). *When Religion Becomes Evil.* New York: HarperCollins Publishers.

Kung, H. (1992). *Judaism: Between Yesterday, and Tomorrow.* New York: Crossroad.

Moyers, B. (2007, October 5). Interview on Christian Zionism with Dr. Timothy P. Weber and Rabbi Michael Lerner. Retrieved May 4, 2008 from www.pbs.org

Olbermann, K. (2009, November 24). Palin talks about her faith. *MSNBC Countdown with Keith Olbermann.* Retrieved November 27, 2009 from www.msnbc.com

Pipes, D. (2003, July 15). Christian Zionism: Israel's best weapon? Retrieved December 31, 2007, from http://christianactionforisrael.org/weapon.html

Schneider, H. (2009, November 17). To two faiths, a holy patch of land; to the world, a powder keg. *The Washington Post.* Retrieved November 27, 2009 from www.washingtonpost.com

Tostevin, M. (2006, September 1). Vatican launches attack on Christian Zionist movement: [Final Edition]. *The Vancouver Sun*, p. A7. Retrieved October 21, 2006, from Canadian Newsstand Core database.

Weber, T. P. (2004). *On the Road to Armageddon: How Evangelicals Became Israel's Best Friend.* Grand Rapids, MI: Baker Academic.

Epilogue: God the Finisher

Hick, J. (2004). *An Interpretation of Religion: Human Responses to the Transcendent.* 2nd edition. New Haven, CT: Yale University Press.

Kung, H. (1980). *Does God Exist? An Answer for Today.* New York: Doubleday.

CPSIA information can be obtained at www.ICGtesting.com
Printed in the USA
LVOW040747290712

291981LV00003B/1/P